People's Knowleuge and
Participatory Action Research

Praise for this book

'*People's Knowledge and Participatory Action Research* offers a radical exploration of the deep knowledge held within communities under siege by neoliberalism and traditional forms of science; the dedicated refusal to surrender this knowledge to the hegemonic gaze of "experts", grip of white supremacy or bribes of corporate interests, and the joy and delicacies of engaging in participatory research for justice. A must-read for community-based researchers and even more so for academics deluded by fantasies of expertise. Congratulations!'
Michelle Fine, Distinguished Professor of Social Psychology,
Women's Studies and Urban Education, City University of New York.

'This book is an important contribution to helping all of us -- academics and grassroots-led researchers -- to think through what it means to collaborate. Clearly written and with both practical wisdom and theoretical reach, it is a book to get some useful conversations started.'
Keri Facer, Professor of Educational & Social Futures,
University of Bristol and AHRC Leadership Fellow, Connected Communities

'Given the pressing environmental and social justice issues facing society today, research should be moving towards a co-production of knowledge with communities. However, too often it is questionable whether it is, or whether there continues to be a top down process of knowledge dissemination to the public from the "white walls" of the academy. Through writing, reflection, poetry and the visual arts, this book draws out these issues -- political, ethical, and social -- and provides an important platform for people outside these walls from which to speak about their collaborative knowledge production practices.'
Jacqueline Vadjunec, Associate Professor,
Department of Geography, Oklahoma State University

'This engrossing and timely collection exposes the weaknesses of conventional academic research. The authors outline a new approach for action research, taking us in a direction that will help heal the many divisions in our fractured world. Anyone involved in research, whether in universities, community organizations or governments, should read it. I loved the fresh voices on gender and race. We should all write letters to our younger action researcher selves acknowledging how colonized we have been. When we liberate ourselves we liberate those with whom we partner. This would be a great deal.'
Hilary Bradbury, Editor of Handbook of
Action Research and Action Research Journal.

People's Knowledge and Participatory Action Research
Escaping the white-walled labyrinth

People's Knowledge Editorial Collective

PRACTICAL ACTION
Publishing

Practical Action Publishing Ltd
The Schumacher Centre,
Bourton on Dunsmore, Rugby,
Warwickshire, CV23 9QZ, UK
www.practicalactionpublishing.org

A catalogue record for this book is available from the British Library.
A catalogue record for this book has been requested from the Library of Congress.

ISBN 978-1-85339-939-8 Hardback
ISBN 978-1-85339-932-9 Paperback
ISBN 978-1-78044-939-5 Library Ebook
ISBN 978-1-78044-932-6 Ebook

Citation: People's Knowledge Editorial Collective (2016) *People's Knowledge and Participatory Action Research: Escaping the white-walled labyrinth*, Rugby, UK: Practical Action Publishing, <http://dx.doi.org/10.3362/9781780449395>.

Since 1974, Practical Action Publishing has published and disseminated books and information in support of international development work throughout the world. Practical Action Publishing is a trading name of Practical Action Publishing Ltd (Company Reg. No. 1159018), the wholly owned publishing company of Practical Action. Practical Action Publishing trades only in support of its parent charity objectives and any profits are covenanted back to Practical Action (Charity Reg. No. 247257, Group VAT Registration No. 880 9924 76).

Front cover photo: *Rara band in Jacmel, Haiti*. From photograph by Richard Fleming, 2015. Original painting by Michel Lafleur.
Cover design by Piers Altman www.piersaitman.co.uk and http://du.st
Typeset by Allzone Digital Services
Printed by Short Run Press Ltd, UK

Further information about the issues covered in this book is available at <http://www.peoplesknowledge.org>.

Contents

List of illustrations vi

Dedication vii

About the People's Knowledge Editorial Collective viii

Acknowledgements ix

Introduction 1

1. Learning at the University of Armageddon 11
   Anonymous contributors

2. Making connections in the 'white-walled labyrinth' 23
   Mayra Guzman, Cedoux Kadima, Grace Lovell, Asha Ali Mohamed,
   Ros Norton, Yosola Olajoye, Federico Rivas and Alpha Thiam

3. Examining our differences 33
   Asha Ali Mohamed, Asma Istwani, Beatriz Villate, Emilia Ohberg,
   Eva Galante, Fatma Mohamed, Ijaba Ahmed, Hinda Mohamed Smith,
   Lucy Pearson, Mayra Guzman, Salma Istwani, Shanti Sakar,
   Susanna Hunter-Darch and Tamanna Miah

4. Cultivating an anti-racist position in post-race society 45
   Jasber Singh

5. Poems 53
   ChriS JaM

6. A puzzling search for authenticity within academia 63
   Lucy Pearson, Javier Sanchez Rodriguez and Asha Ali Mohamed

7. Community media and cultural politics on Tyneside 73
   Hugh Kelly with Graham Jeffery

8. A civil rights activist reflects on research 83
   David Clay

9. LIVErNORTH: combining individual and collective
   patient knowledge 93
   Tilly Hale

10. The original citizen scientists 103
    People's Knowledge Editorial Collective with paintings
    from Haiti by Michel Lafleur

11. Signposts for people's knowledge 113
    Tom Wakeford

Glossary 135

Index 143

http://dx.doi.org/10.3362/9781780449395.000

List of illustrations

BlueJam (Onashile Artists)   53

Charlemagne Peralte, leader of the Cacos rebellion against the American invasion of Haiti in 1915 (Lafleur)   104

Peasant woman collecting tree roots for making charcoal (Lafleur)   104

Claude Casseus, ghetto author from the Grand Rue neighbourhood, Port-au-Prince, Haiti (Lafleur)   105

Fishing boat off the shores of Leogane, Haiti (Lafleur)   106

Maurice Semilos, carpenter and furniture maker from Ghetto Leanne, Port-au-Prince, Haiti   106

Joseph Ducaste, Tap Tap driver and mechanic from the Grand Rue neighbourhood, Port-au-Prince, Haiti   107

Boss Thelius Simeon, independent tailor off Boulevard Jean-Jaques Desalines, Port-au-Prince, Haiti (Lafleur)   108

Peasant coffee producer in Cayes Jacmel, Haiti (Lafleur)   108

Rara band in Jacmel, Haiti (Lafleur)   109

Bebe, chef and restaurateur, 'Soutie Bon Griot' restaurant in Montrouis, Haiti (Lafleur)   111

Dedicated to the memory of our co-author,
Tilly Hale (1943–2015)

Co-published by Practical Action Publishing and the Centre for Agroecology, Water and Resilience (CAWR), Coventry University

The Centre for Agroecology, Water and Resilience (CAWR) is driving innovative, transdisciplinary research on the understanding and development of socially just and resilient food and water systems internationally. Unique to this University Research Centre is the incorporation of citizen-generated knowledge - the participation of farmers, water users and other citizens in transdisciplinary research, using holistic approaches which cross many disciplinary boundaries among the humanities as well as the natural and social sciences.

Centre for Agroecology, Water and Resilience (CAWR)
Coventry University
Ryton Gardens, Wolston Lane,
Coventry, CV8 3LG, United Kingdom.

E-mail: CAWROffice@coventry.ac.uk
Tel: +44 (0) 2477 651 601
Web: www.coventry.ac.uk/cawr

The *Reclaiming Diversity and Citizenship Series* seeks to encourage debate outside mainstream policy and conceptual frameworks towards an equitable and sustainable future based on social and ecological diversity, human rights, and more inclusive forms of citizenship. Contributors to the *Reclaiming Diversity and Citizenship Series* are encouraged to reflect deeply on their ways of working and outcomes of their research, highlighting implications for policy, knowledge, organisations, and practice.

The *Reclaiming Diversity and Citizenship Series* was published by the International Institute for Environment and Development (IIED) between 2006 and 2013. The Series is now published by the Centre for Agroecology, Water and Resilience, at Coventry University.

Professor Michel Pimbert is the coordinator and editor of the *Reclaiming Diversity and Citizenship Series*. The views expressed in this volume are those of the authors and do not necessarily reflect the views of the Centre for Agroecology, Water and Resilience, its partners and donors.

About the People's Knowledge Editorial Collective

The People's Knowledge Editorial Collective includes pioneering and award-winning practitioners of participatory action research and other critical approaches to knowledge co-production. They have worked with a range of organizations and individuals that have attempted participatory and inclusive approaches to undertaking research, including the Mayor of London, Greenpeace, Joseph Rowntree Foundation, the International School of Bottom-up Organizing, Nomad, European Commission and UK Research Councils.

Acknowledgements

The period during which we developed this book saw the death of the beloved father of Hinda Mohamed Smith, who was a great influence and inspiration. As a collective, we would like to pay tribute to him.

We are indebted to the Arts and Humanities Research Council, which funded the initial project that brought many of us together – Web of Connections. We would particularly like to thank Roshni Abidin, Paul McWhirter, Gary Grubb, Keri Facer, Jill Mustard, George McKay and all those in the Connected Communities programme. We are also grateful to the participants in a workshop funded under this programme that focused on the ethics of researchers working with communities. These included Jacky Birrane, Ali Campbell, Tina Cook, Iman Ahmed, Katja Frimberger, Abera Ghirmay, Anne Jay, Susanne Kean, Sarah Keyes, Taylor Love, Ismail Mohamed, Alison Phipps, Jackie Sands, Rose Sharp, Gameli Tordzro, Howard Turner, Erin Walcon, Jean Winter, and Paul Winter.

At Sheffield University, Kimberley Marwood undertook a very helpful copy-edit of all the chapters.

At Edinburgh University, we are indebted to Nisha Patel, Charlotte Clarke, Heather Wilkinson, Brenda Saetta, and Sarah Keyes.

We received vital encouragement from Lisa Cumming, Kerrie Schaeffer, Linda McKie, Lisa Matthews, Alison Phipps, as well as Rachel Pain and Susan Frenk at Durham University, who helped us organize a key workshop and offered even more. We are also indebted to Ann Light at Sussex University, Tracey Robbins, Alex O'Neil, and Emma Stone of the Joseph Rowntree Foundation.

Each member of our editorial collective is embedded within a wider web of advice and support.

Hinda Mohamed Smith: I would like to thank my husband, Phill Smith, for his endless support, love, and encouragement during this project, and my son, Aydan Nesta Smith, for being the most content baby ever – we love you. My thanks extend to the rest of my family and friends for their continued support and love.

Javier Sanchez Rodriguez: I would like to thank all the young people in RefugeeYouth with whom I have worked over the years; they all have always been a source of inspiration for me. Thanks go also to my partner, Maria, and my children, Chia and Mallkum, for being patient with me while I worked on this project.

Chris Nelson (aka JaM): I would like to thank my fellow editors who have fed mind without starving heart, nor shut the door to art's power to enrich and edutain. To my family, particularly my wife Rachael, for unwavering support and unconditional love. And to my mother, Alexia Nelson, who left us just before publication of this book. Wishing her Pan-like grand adventures in more vivid realms. To the whole team, to the whole and the as yet unknown.

Nicole Kenton: My gratitude goes to Tom and all the editors for taking me on this insightful journey. I also thank my family – my partner, Steve, and our children, Adam, Ruben, and Livia – for their support and encouragement, as always.

Tom Wakeford: I would like to thank all the other editors and my family, particularly Fiona Hale, who continued to support me in this project, despite personal illness and the loss of our beloved Tilly. And Laura, who was patient while I spent time staring at a screen.

Our Editorial Collective has been supported by staff at the Centre for Agro-ecology, Water and Resilience, Coventry University, in particular by Carole Fox, Layla Riches, Mina Thompson, Jane Batey, Liz Woodard, Marina Plunkett, and Michel Pimbert. It has been hosted by the People's Knowledge and Trans-disciplinarity Working Group, with the support of Colin Anderson and Chiara Tornaghi.

Finally, we are very grateful for the constructive feedback from Jacqueline Vadjunec and two anonymous reviewers. All errors and omissions are, however, our own.

Introduction

People's Knowledge Editorial Collective

Abstract

This is a brief survey of the key themes in the book, particularly the relationship between knowledge and power. It explores how a person's race, class, gender, sexuality, health status or disability, a lack of formal training, or a different mode of expression, can all prevent their insights from being accepted as potentially valid. It introduces participatory action research, which allows greater equality between such people and professionally trained experts in the research process.

Keywords: participatory action research, experts, power, knowledge, racism

> 'The most potent weapon in the hands of the oppressor is the mind of the oppressed.' (Steve Biko, anti-apartheid activist, 1946–77)

> 'What I propose, therefore, is very simple: it is nothing more than to think what we are doing.' (Hannah Arendt, philosopher, 1906–75)

Knowledge and justice

Every second, people across the world are generating new ideas and wise insights. In some cases such understanding is harnessed in collective or individual efforts to promote justice, health, and the well-being of ourselves and our environment. At the times when it is most needed, however, this vast realm of knowledge is usually left languishing in obscurity. Worse, as in some of the last century's most famous cases of healthcare failure, toxic pollution, and other human rights abuses, it is sometimes actively suppressed.

A person's race, class, gender, sexuality, health status or disability, a lack of formal training, or a different mode of expression, can all prevent their insights from being accepted as potentially valid. The expertise people gain from life experience is routinely ignored by professionals, even those whose job it is to engage with such people. Miranda Fricker (2007) has named this as 'epistemic injustice' (see Glossary). To make matters worse, people's insights can be obscured and distorted by sections of the media and by others in positions of authority. Together they form an institutionalized system of discrimination.

Our aim in this collection of essays is to unpack some of these processes of discrimination, which appear to be endemic in research carried out at universities and a wide range of other research institutions. We also aim to provide pointers to a future in which we can better address the unjust and nonsensical hierarchies

http://dx.doi.org/10.3362/9781780449395.001

that exist, for example, between formally trained researchers and grassroots-based researchers who draw expertise from experience, or between those of us trained in countries that are dominated by white people compared to those working in the Global South (see Glossary). Questioning these hierarchies – striving for what Indian analyst Shiv Visvanathan calls 'cognitive justice' (see Glossary) – involves struggling with one's own identity as a thinking being, as contributions in the following pages reveal.

When those of us who live our lives outside a university setting come across the concept of research, so many ideas come to mind: being academic guinea pigs, statistics, knowledge, data, analysis, hypothesis, theory, science, subject/object, complexity, language, accessibility, (mis)understanding, colonialism, and men with bow ties and white coats. It is 'them', not 'us'.

Maori scholar-activist Linda Tuhiwai Smith (2012) points out that many people whose ancestors have been colonized or enslaved have a negative attitude to the word 'research'. For them 'the word itself is probably one of the dirtiest words in the indigenous world's vocabulary', she writes; 'it is implicated in the worst excesses of colonialism'. For many people who are descended from those who were oppressed by what they saw as a scientific rationale for running an immoral system, science itself is tainted (see Wakeford, 2016; Chilisa, 2012).

We propose that all humans are potential researchers and that this is an innate human quality that we all possess. Approaches such as 'participatory action research' (PAR – see Glossary) and the principle of doing research inclusively (Nind, 2014) put people from the non-dominant groups in society, like many of the authors here, at the centre of the research process. No longer the subject of research, we become researchers on things that concern us and on which we have gained expertise through our experience. PAR recognizes that we are all able to utilize a range of methodologies to investigate, analyse, reflect on, and come to terms with new knowledge. Furthermore these processes of inquiry have the potential to help us overcome the forces that oppress us.

People's Knowledge and Participatory Action Research is an attempt to document and critically examine some of the different steps involved when embarking on a collaborative research project. As contributors to this book, we came together out of a common interest in justice and in having our understanding of the world respected. Each of us brings our own perspectives on the production and validation of new knowledge to the edited volume we present here.

Whether we are based in non-governmental organizations, social movements, or universities, we have all had experiences of our knowledge – or that of our collaborators – being devalued or excluded by those with the power to do so. We decided to come together in a series of workshops during the period 2012–15. We invited other, more privileged researchers, who have received formal research training (and who regularly receive recognition in the form of funding and publishing of their analyses), to join us. Aiming to explore how we might work together better in the future, we shared our differently situated perspectives. We concluded that, to achieve our objective, we must first document and provide a road map of what is going wrong in the way research is done at present.

The financial support for our initial meetings came about with the UK's research funding councils attempting to support what has variously been called 'participatory research', 'community engagement', 'citizen science', 'action research', and the 'co-production' of knowledge (see Glossary for an insight into these terms). All these buzz phrases are heard with increasing frequency in academic and policy circles (e.g. Facer and Enright, 2016; Durose and Richardson, 2016; Etmanski et al., 2014). However, first-hand testimonies by those who have taken part in such processes are extremely difficult to find (but see Drame and Irby, 2015; Pearce, 2010; Walmsley et al. 2013). This publication is an attempt to contribute towards filling this gap.

Of the five people in our editorial collective, only one (Wakeford) has undergone formal postgraduate training or led an academically funded research project. The lead authors of all except one chapter (Wakeford, 2016) are from the world outside academia. Although most of us are not professionally trained, we believe that our lived experience gives us a perspective that is a useful complement to that of academic professionals. However well-intentioned, such experts often lack a depth and/or breadth of knowledge of that which they study.

The participation industry's buzz phrases, along with approaches such as PAR, have risen to prominence at a time when the training and daily lives of professional researchers rarely include spaces in which they (and for some of us this should say 'we') can think morally, historically, or philosophically. In *The Human Condition*, which explored the challenge of acting ethically in the post-Holocaust world, Hannah Arendt writes: 'What I propose, therefore, is very simple: it is nothing more than to think what we are doing' (1998). The 11 chapters here illustrate Arendt's advice that, if we are to understand what we mean by research, science, and participation, we are required to really 'think' about our actions. As she was a philosopher and historian, it is clear that what she meant was we need to think, not in some vague general sense, but rather to use historical perspective and philosophical analysis.

As you read each of the chapters that follow, we suggest that you, the reader, think about your responses to the following questions, which we, the editorial collective, have put to the authors:

1. What kinds of difficulties arise when people from non-dominant back-grounds or oppressed groups in society work with professional research-ers to achieve positive social change?
2. What changes will be required to ensure that new knowledge and under-standing is generated, in a spirit of respectful dialogue between people whose collaboration takes place on an equal footing?
3. How can we work together to imagine future initiatives and allianc-es that could bring about an authentic 'people's knowledge'? These initiatives would privilege neither the professional researcher nor those

whose expertise comes from their life experience, neither white people nor people of colour, neither women nor men, and so on.

Overview of the chapters

Following the maxim that we learn more from reflecting on failure than on triumphs, the contribution entitled 'Learning at the University of Armageddon' (Anonymous contributors, 2016) arose from an open call for experiences from community groups, funders, artists, and researchers about the many ways in which attempts by communities to work with powerful institutions can fail. In a similar vein, Chapter 2 (Guzman et al., 2016), written by members of RefugeeYouth, is a set of reflections on a collaborative project with academics that attempted to implement PAR approaches on a large scale.

Historically, academia has been, in the words of Yancy (1998: 8–9), 'white men engaged in conversation with themselves'. We could add that these white men have tended to be heterosexual, able-bodied, and from well-off backgrounds. The 'white-walled labyrinth' of our subtitle is taken from Chapter 2, in which the authors quote Leonard Harris's observation that: 'the [academic] works of Afro-Americans are trapped, as it were, in a labyrinth where even the walls are white' (Harris, 1983, in Brookfield, 2005: 275). His analysis applies just as much to the attempts of mainstream academia to undertake projects using participation and co-produced knowledge as it does to non-participatory research.

Even if intended as an intellectual project for the liberation of all humankind, participatory research's location in the discourses of the dominant groups in society means that it may well function as yet one more of what Yancy calls a 'site of white cultural hegemony, sustained and perpetuated in terms of the particularity of race and gender-related institutional power' (Yancy, 1998: 3).

Many of us who have taken part in the initiatives described here are from backgrounds that contain multiple elements of disadvantage or oppression. Rather than conducting an 'oppression Olympics' and declaring race the winner of the 'most oppressed' category, the phrase 'white-walled labyrinth' can act as a symbol of the wide range of other identities and backgrounds that can lead to people's oppression.

In order to support attempts at human flourishing, we believe that research should be participatory and embrace different types of knowledge and self-expression.

Several chapters argue the need to critically think about 'race' when conducting action research projects. For example, where does the power lie within the structure we are working in, who is talking about whom, and who has the power? This is evident from Chapter 2 (Guzman et al., 2016), when RefugeeYouth started working with academic institutes. In the funding application, the people of colour were the case study material and the white people were the researchers and co-researchers. This was not RefugeeYouth's first experience of engaging with the issue of race. Its members continue to engage with the issues raised by skin colour and they have now come to recognize that white privilege is institutional rather than merely personal.

In Chapter 3, Mohamed and her co-authors (2016) uncover the multiple challenges raised by both race and gender. They describe the evolution of a space for women from different backgrounds, with different experiences of gender injustice and inequality, where they can share their stories and work together with men to 'create a world where sexism doesn't exist'. Singh's (2016) contribution (Chapter 4) points to a major challenge to doing research inclusively (Nind, 2014) and knowledge co-production, which is the denial that institutionalized and cultural racism still exists in countries such as the UK. Singh suggests that 'doing action research without critically engaging with [racism] is likely to reinforce racist and colonial positions'.

Approaches such as PAR can, when conducted properly, unearth inherent tensions around representation, identity, power, and the nature of knowledge itself. In some cases, it can lead to disobedience by communities, a refusal to walk along traditional academic lines in an attempt to ensure that different types of knowledge and self-expression are valued equally. Power imbalances can sometimes be redressed. Pearson and co-authors employ one such strategy in Chapter 6 (Pearson et al., 2016), where they resist an invitation to write an academic paper by giving good reasons why they should not write one. Singh (2016) builds on this argument in Chapter 4, in which he explores three overlapping ideas in the context of action research and race: firstly, recognizing the dominant position of racism in our culture; secondly, recognizing race as an experience; and thirdly, the need for an ongoing process of decolonizing our thinking. Action research can play a key role in challenging the issues that are raised in this publication.

Community film-maker Hugh Kelly collaborated with academic Graham Jeffery (2016) to write Chapter 7, a commentary on a film building on 30 years of participatory research using video in northern England. Many of the characters in it are from white working-class backgrounds, themselves oppressed by the neoliberal policies of governments from 1979 onwards, particularly the mass unemployment and waste of human talent that began in the Thatcher era – epitomized by the miners' strike of 1984–5.

Whilst Kelly uses film as an alternative to the written word, another strategy of breaking out of the academic labyrinth, used by JaM (2016), is to communicate complex ideas through theatre or poetry. We let these speak, in the case of JaM literally, for themselves (Chapter 5).

David Clay's (2016) and Tilly Hale's (2016) chapters are first-person accounts. Clay is an acute analyst of racism in modern Britain, and in Liverpool in particular, through his experience co-producing a community newsletter focusing on the 'black experience' (Chapter 8). Though he may not be regarded by professionally trained researchers as one of them, his experience as a leader in Liverpool's civil rights movement gives this chapter, and its accompanying filmed interview, an authority that puts many academic studies of the same subject in the shade. The late Tilly Hale, to whom this book is dedicated, describes the progress that can be made when health researchers recognize the expertise of patients living with chronic disease (Chapter 9).

In Chapter 10 (People's Knowledge Editorial Collective, 2016), we present Lafleur's paintings and a short essay in response to 'the rise of the role of "citizen scientist" ' amongst dominant groups in Europe, Australia, and North America. Citizen science has become prominent in some scientific circles and is a term that has entered the mainstream via the media as a magic bullet for societal problems. To understand how we got to the present day, the chapter challenges us to think about citizen science in its real historical context – not the sanitized version most high school and undergraduate scientists are taught.

In Europe and North America, universities are increasingly subject to neoliberal governance. Academics must meet funding and publication goals. For those of us who are professional researchers, the duties to our fellow citizens often fall by the wayside because we are employed by, and subject to the rules of, institutions whose policies are actively undermining democracy. Science research bodies now talk of citizen science, whilst simultaneously devaluing the political rights of citizens.

In her book *Undoing the Demos*, Wendy Brown (2015) suggests that, for the policymakers who implement neoliberalism, humans are only and everywhere *homo economicus*, to the exclusion of *homo politicus*. The political concept of the citizen was developed through Ancient Greece and Rome, the French Revolution, various anti-colonial struggles, and the US civil rights movement. When this political dimension of being human is extinguished, says Brown, 'it takes with it the necessary energies, practices, and culture of democracy, as well as its very intelligibility'. Where there are only marketplaces, the demos, hence the citizens, do not exist.

Business models and metrics have come to irrigate every crevice of society, circulating from investment banks to schools, from corporations to universities, from public agencies to the individual. It is through the replacement of democratic terms of law, participation, and justice with idioms of benchmarks, objectives, and buy-ins that governance dismantles democratic life whilst appearing only to instil it with 'best practices'.

This book marks a deliberate blurring of the boundaries between academia and grassroots-led research. The different approaches here serve, we hope, to deepen our collective dialogue on these issues. We envisage a future in which we will be able to appreciate different kinds of knowledge, using participatory methods in a wide range of contexts, such as poetry, film, archaeology, theatre, and literature. Each would enable people to have a voice to challenge the world around them in the pursuit of social justice.

Escaping the labyrinth together

We note that several commentators who are most pessimistic about the future of participatory approaches (e.g. Cooke and Kothari, 2001; Miessen, 2010) publish their thoughts in places where the only likely audience will be their fellow academics. In contrast, we feel there is a moral imperative for such critics to enter public spaces and work with grassroots-based researchers to improve PAR and approaches which share its values. To this end we have made the electronic version of this book open access, reduced academic jargon to a bare minimum and compiled a Glossary at the end of the book. This contains thumbnail working definitions of some key terms that might be useful, particularly for communities without access to the resources that lie behind university paywalls.

In the grassroots-based struggles in which all the authors in this book are active (some or all of the time), critiques are only useful if they help us reflect on, and thereby improve, our actions. University-based researchers willing to join us in these cycles of reflection and action are not easy to find, but they do exist. In Chapter 11, Tom Wakeford (2016) offers some provisional signposts for us on this collaborative journey.

As well as supporting learning amongst people without formal research training, we hope that this book serves as a resource to allow professional researchers, particularly those from dominant groups in society, to reflect on their own practice.

After his trial for playing a key role in facilitating and managing the logistics of mass deportation of Jews to ghettos and extermination camps, Adolf Eichmann was widely described as evil. In her book, *Eichmann in Jerusalem* (1963), Hannah Arendt coined the phrase 'the banality of evil' to describe Eichmann. Her point was that Eichmann was not a fanatic or sociopath, but rather an average person who relied on clichéd defences rather than thinking for himself. He was motivated by professional advancement rather than being an ideological zealot. Banality, in this sense, is not that Eichmann's actions in helping carry out the mass extermination of 20 million people were ordinary, or that there is a potential Eichmann in all of us, but that his actions were motivated by a sort of stupidity which was, and sadly is, wholly unexceptional.

Arendt never denied that Eichmann was an anti-Semite, nor that he was fully responsible for his actions, but argued that these characteristics were secondary to his stupidity. To the question of whether Eichmann was evil she answered, 'No, he was just a schmuck'. 'Schmuck' has its origins in Yiddish and means a foolish, obnoxious, contemptible, or detestable person.

Michelle Fine, a PAR practitioner and teacher in the USA, watched the recent docudrama about Arendt's encounter with Eichmann as she travelled to the UK during the course of this book's preparation. At a conference the day after, she challenged her audience to assess the extent to which researchers who fail to reflect on their actions, and thus ignore the humanity of their research subjects, are in fact evil. She feared that some of them/us in research institutions will continue to add words like participatory, or phrases such as citizen science, to their/our grant applications, without reflecting on what they/we are really doing (see Arendt's quote opening this chapter).

We do not doubt the sincere desire many professional researchers have to do good. Neither does Fine. Yet, in collaborating with governments that Henry Giroux (2013) accuses of carrying out a new eugenics of neoliberalism (see

Glossary), and in their/our continued failure to speak out against the dominant systems of oppression, particularly the injustice and institutionalized racism in research institutions, they/we risk being consigned to history as, in Arendt's sense, 'schmucks'.

Neither research institutions nor individual researchers can alone bring about the changes needed to develop a people's knowledge. As we attempt to reform the structures that oppress some of us, and thus by extension oppress all of us on some level, we dedicate this book to cultivating better collaborations between professional researchers and those based in social movements.

Many academics working in relevant areas consider such movements uncritical, chaotic, or unrepresentative. Comments we have recently heard from academic colleagues include: 'we need research, not activism', 'we're a research centre, not a protest group'; questions they raised include: 'who do these activists represent?' and 'what's the point of writing a book that is for people outside universities?' Whilst it may be that some social movements are not self-critical enough, and can suffer from periods during which there are apparent lacks of effective organization or mechanisms of accountability, all these things can also be said of academic institutions.

Only by entering into closer dialogue can professional researchers and those involved in grassroots-led campaigns or social movements generate useful knowledge. We pay tribute to the collective efforts to this end of all those who contributed to this book, and commit ourselves to attempts to escape the white-walled labyrinth by continuing the struggle.

References

Anonymous contributors (2016) 'Learning at the University of Armageddon', in People's Knowledge Editorial Collective (eds), *People's Knowledge and Participatory Action Research: Escaping the White-Walled Labyrinth*, pp. 11–22, Practical Action Publishing, Rugby <http://dx.doi.org/10.3362/9781780449395.002>.

Arendt, H. (1963) *Eichmann in Jerusalem: A Report on the Banality of Evil*, Penguin, New York, NY; Chicago, IL.

Arendt, H. (1998) *The Human Condition*, 2nd rev. edn, University of Chicago Press, Chicago, IL.

Brookfield, S. (2005) *The Power of Critical Theory for Adult Learning and Teaching*, Open University Press, New York, NY.

Brown, W. (2015) *Undoing the Demos: Neoliberalism's Stealth Revolution*, MIT Press, Cambridge, MA.

Chilisa, B. (2012) *Indigenous Research Methodologies*, Sage Publishing, London.

Clay, D. (2016) 'A civil rights activist reflects on research', in People's Knowledge Editorial Collective (eds), *People's Knowledge and Participatory Action Research: Escaping the White-Walled Labyrinth*, pp. 83–92, Practical Action Publishing, Rugby <http://dx.doi.org/10.3362/9781780449395.009>.

Cooke, B. and Kothari, U. (2001) *Participation: The New Tyranny?* Zed Books, London.

Drame, D. and Irby, D. (2015) *Black Participatory Research: Power, Identity, and the Struggle for Justice in Education*, Palgrave Macmillan, New York, NY.

Durose, C. and Richardson, L. (2016) *Designing Public Policy for Co-production: Theory, Practice and Change*, Policy Press, Bristol.

Etmanski, C., Hall, B. and Dawson, T. (eds) (2014) *Learning and Teaching Community-based Research: Linking Pedagogy to Practice*, University of Toronto Press, Toronto.

Facer, K. and Enright, B. (2016) *Creating Living Knowledge: The Connected Communities Programme, Community University Relationships and the Participatory Turn in the Production of Knowledge*, University of Bristol/AHRC Connected Communities, Bristol.

Fricker, M. (2007) *Epistemic Injustice: Power and the Ethics of Knowing*, Oxford University Press, Oxford.

Giroux, H.A. (2013) 'The occupy movement meets the suicidal state: neoliberalism and the punishing of dissent', *Situations: Project of the Radical Imagination*, 5: 7–34 <http://ojs.gc.cuny.edu/index.php/situations/article/viewFile/1432/1467> [accessed 3 August 2016].

Guzman, M., Kadima, C., Lovell, G., Mohamed, A.A., Norton, R., Rivas, F. and Thiam, A. (2016) 'Making connections in the "white-walled labyrinth"', in People's Knowledge Editorial Collective (eds), *People's Knowledge and Participatory Action Research: Escaping the White-Walled Labyrinth*, pp. 23–32, Practical Action Publishing, Rugby <http://dx.doi.org/10.3362/9781780449395.003>.

Hale, T. (2016) 'LIVErNORTH: combining individual and collective patient knowledge', in People's Knowledge Editorial Collective (eds), *People's Knowledge and Participatory Action Research: Escaping the White-Walled Labyrinth*, pp. 93–102, Practical Action Publishing, Rugby <http://dx.doi.org/10.3362/9781780449395.010>.

JaM, C. (2016) 'Poems', in People's Knowledge Editorial Collective (eds), *People's Knowledge and Participatory Action Research: Escaping the White-Walled Labyrinth*, pp. 53–62, Practical Action Publishing, Rugby <http://dx.doi.org/10.3362/9781780449395.006>.

Kelly, H. with Jeffery, G. (2016) 'Community media and cultural politics on Tyneside', in People's Knowledge Editorial Collective (eds), *People's Knowledge and Participatory Action Research: Escaping the White-Walled Labyrinth*, pp. 73–82, Practical Action Publishing, Rugby <http://dx.doi.org/10.3362/9781780449395.008>.

Miessen, M. (2010) *The Nightmare of Participation*, Sternberg Press, New York, NY.

Mohamed, A.A., Istwani, A., Villate, B., Ohberg, E., Galante, E., Mohamed, F., Ahmed, I., Smith, H.M., Pearson, L., Guzman, M., Istwani, S., Sakar, S., Hunter-Darch, S. and Miah, T. (2016) 'Examining our differences', in People's Knowledge Editorial Collective (eds), *People's Knowledge and Participatory Action Research: Escaping the White-Walled Labyrinth*, pp. 35–46, Practical Action Publishing, Rugby <http://dx.doi.org/10.3362/9781780449395.004>.

Nind, M. (2014) *What is Inclusive Research?*, The 'What is?' research method series, Bloomsbury Publishing, London and New York, NY.

Pearce, J. (2010) *Participation and Democracy in the Twenty-First Century City*, Springer, Dordrecht.

Pearson, L., Sanchez Rodriguez, J. and Mohamed, A.A. (2016) 'A puzzling search for authenticity within academia', in People's Knowledge Editorial Collective (eds) *People's Knowledge and Participatory Action Research: Escaping the White-Walled Labyrinth*, pp. 63–72, Practical Action Publishing, Rugby <http://dx.doi.org/10.3362/9781780449395.007>.

People's Knowledge Editorial Collective (2016) 'The original citizen scientists', in People's Knowledge Editorial Collective (eds), *People's
Knowledge and Participatory Action Research: Escaping the White-Walled Labyrinth*, pp. 103–112, Practical Action Publishing, Rugby <http://dx.doi.
org/10.3362/9781780449395.011 >.

Singh, J. (2016) 'Cultivating an anti-racist position in post-race society', in People's Knowledge Editorial Collective (eds), *People's Knowledge and Participatory Action Research: Escaping the White-Walled Labyrinth*, pp. 45–52, Practical
Action Publishing, Rugby <http://dx.doi.org/10.3362/9781780449395.005>.

Tuhiwai Smith, L. (2012) *Decolonizing Methodologies: Research and Indigenous
Peoples*, 2nd edn, Zed Books, London.

Wakeford, T. (2016) 'Signposts for people's knowledge', in People's Knowl-
edge Editorial Collective (eds), *People's Knowledge and Participatory Action
Research: Escaping the White-Walled Labyrinth*, pp. 113–134, Practical Action
Publishing, Rugby <http://dx.doi.org/10.3362/9781780449395.012>.

Walmsley, J., Davies, C., Hales, M. and Flux, R. (eds) (2013) *Better Health in
Harder Times: Active Citizens and Innovation on the Front Line*, Policy Press,
Bristol.

Yancy, G. (ed.) (1998) *African-American Philosophers: 17 Conversations*, Routledge, New York, NY.

About the authors

The People's Knowledge Editorial Collective jointly authored this introduction.
They are **Nicole Kenton, Hinda Mohamed Smith, Chris Nelson, Javier
Sanchez Rodriguez**, and **Tom Wakeford.**

CHAPTER 1

Learning at the University of Armageddon

Anonymous contributors

Abstract

Who documents the difficulties and obstacles encountered when non-academics collaborate with academics in the pursuit of social justice? This chapter is a compilation of responses to an open call for people to submit, anonymously, stories of negative experiences of working with universities. People from diverse backgrounds, including grassroots activists, researchers, and a funding officer, briefly documented their experiences, and the chapter reflects on and aims to learn from their responses to the call.

Keywords: co-production, collaborative research, tokenism, social justice, research council

Introduction

There was no golden age of universities, at least in the UK. The silencing of voices that speak against the mainstream began long before the last decade when universities embraced neoliberalism. Prime Minister Harold Wilson established a new wave of higher education institutions in the 1960s. It saw a dozen new universities set up across the country that were meant to foster radical thinking and promote social justice. But those put in charge of many of these institutions often could not stand critical thinkers, for fear that they might stir up trouble. Those who taught in the traditions of Paulo Freire, or who sympathized with those who did, were sometimes quietly removed from their positions.

University managements have been accused of eroding the freedom of their researchers, as most academics are coerced into publishing in highly specialized publications that often filter out elements – if there were any present – that might help people take action on issues of injustice. Less widely known is the paradox whereby many universities are using the language of public engagement, community participation, and collaborative inquiry for the public good, whilst at the same time preventing schemes that might allow research to take place inclusively. This happens at the same time as researchers feel under increasing pressure to publish only 'successful' research, whereas in the real world everyone knows that we learn much more from mistakes than triumphs. Combined with the pressure to produce

http://dx.doi.org/10.3362/9781780449395.002

'results' – and on a timescale that does not allow good relationships to develop between researchers in academic institutions and those who work outside their walls – these tendencies risk making the barriers between these groups insurmountable.

This chapter is a compilation of responses to an open call, as part of the UK Arts and Humanities Research Council's Connected Communities programme, for people to submit, anonymously, stories of negative experiences to a fictional institution named the University of Armageddon. Our aim is to reflect on and learn from the eight vignettes that resulted from this call. People from diverse backgrounds, including grassroots activists, participatory (and non-participatory) researchers, and even funders, wrote the following short accounts of their experiences. Some names have been changed.

Not refugee enough

Inspired by the experience of attending a research council symposium, we jumped at the opportunity to submit an abstract to an international conference held by Oxford University's Refugee Studies Centre entitled *Refugee Voices*. This conference promised to take a new perspective on refugee issues, giving voice to the real lived experiences of people with refugee backgrounds. We found it refreshing to hear about a conference that was concerned with the voices of people from refugee communities as well as the voices of academic researchers. This resonated deeply with us as, in our experience, young people from refugee backgrounds are always expected to be the subject of research rather than the authors of their own knowledge.

We submitted an abstract which focused on exploring power, representation, and voice, looking at: the extent to which the voices of individuals/ groups of people who are from refugee communities are being heard in the academic world; to what degree these communities have control of how they are defined and represented; and the analysis of their experiences.

We were delighted that our abstract was selected for presentation at the conference, but were unable to attend because we were expected to pay a fee to do so. The negotiations with Oxford University that ensued were frustrating. They failed to recognize the importance of our collective research approach, and were only interested in one 'author' coming to present. Eventually, the University conceded and said that we could attend just to present our own workshop, but could not go to the rest of the conference. We initially agreed to this, but later declined when they started making intrusive demands about people's immigration status and identification documents. We felt that they had missed the point of our contribution entirely, which was all about how important it is not to define people by their immigration status, and how being a refugee is an experience – and not necessarily an identity people want displayed in public. The experience highlighted for us the difficulty of trying to engage with an academic world which is very closed and exclusive.

Collaborative research for social injustice

One day, a group of academics started circulating an invitation to other professionally trained researchers as well as to people whose expertise came from practical experience as researchers and activists in their communities. Would they like to write something about what it was like when communities tried to generate knowledge alongside academics? They were asked to write a short summary – the so-called abstract. If this were accepted they would be paid a modest fee to write 2,000 words, and be invited to a workshop at which they would meet academic researchers. Together they would write a book, which would be available for free.

Jan was a retired community-based worker on social justice issues. They had built up considerable knowledge of a particular local area. In these streets, and in the city more generally, they were respected by the whole community, even by those with whom they had been in dispute over the years. They refereed for a local football team as a way of bringing excluded local youth together. An excellent writer, they submitted an abstract and it was accepted. They then wrote the longer article for the book and turned up with anticipation to the event, held at a country hotel.

The workshop included eight people from community and activist backgrounds and 20 academics. The organiser had never hosted such a mixed group before. As soon as the workshop got underway it was clear that the academic style of discussion was going to dominate. Even the 'getting-to-know-you' game involved a competitive element, as to who had brought the most interesting object to represent their work.

Despite most of the professional academic participants having had little or no experience of working on equal terms with collaborators whose expertise came from practical experience, they were paired up with them to discuss their respective papers. The common theme of the book was meant to be 'co-production of knowledge for social justice', but the way people interpreted this brief was left to them.

From debriefing with them afterwards, the community-based experts-through-experience did not, as a rule, feel valued by this process. Their experiential knowledge was often viewed as mere anecdote. Their lack of background in academic theory meant they lacked the vocabulary and conceptual tools to discuss the work in a way the academics found interesting. Their practical expertise in undertaking community-based research was ignored or even denigrated.

At one point the workshop leader suggested that everyone should think about their contribution in terms of how it related to 'theories of change'. It came across as implying that activists don't think, they just act. Yet Jan had demonstrated that they, along with the members of the civil rights movement in which he was immersed, did have a theory of change, as they had used one to achieve some of their desires for change. Another participant was an action researcher involved in regional social movements in Latin America.

The academics present gained esteem from attending the event, particularly as it was sponsored by a research council. They used the event for networking with each other, scoping out future collaborations and discussing new grant proposals. Lacking a professional status or institution, non-academics were not in a position to use the meeting for these purposes.

Community-based experts had come on the understanding that the meeting was a necessary stage in a process that would lead to their contribution being published in a book – one that would be of interest to community activists and other non-academics involved in grassroots-led research projects. Yet, as the meeting came to a close and discussion turned to the event's outputs, it became clear that this original objective had been jettisoned. Jan took part in a final plenary session, during which they were involved in the following exchange with two of the event's academic organizers, Dan and Bobby.

> Jan: 'I have not understood most of the discussion here. Lots of long academic words have been used that mean nothing to me. I understood that we were here to get a book produced. Is that still the plan?'

> Dan: [ignoring Jan] 'I think it's becoming clear that there is interest in producing a book as a guide on how to do co-produced research – a guide for the next generation of researchers.'

> Bobby: 'By this I hope we mean a guide aimed at being useful to the whole of the next generation of researchers, not just PhD students. Otherwise, where is the social justice?'

> Dan: 'C'mon, Bobby – get real!'

In subsequent discussion and emails following the workshop Dan made clear that the audience for the book would be early-career academics: PhD students and others working at the postgraduate level. It would be published by a traditional academic publisher and would not be free. None of the community-based researchers or activists were approached about having their contributions included, nor were they involved in the editing process. To the best of our knowledge, no non-academics were involved in the publication process. Yet everything that took place at the meeting was undertaken using public money, on the basis that community-based researchers and academics were going to collaborate together.

Stories from a funder's perspective

I worked at a senior level for one of the top three largest providers of grants of social research in the UK for many years. On a different day I might theme these stories slightly differently. There's an infinite way of cutting the cake, but the essential tastes and ingredients are there. These are my experiences. Different funders or managers might have different experiences ... and some of them are as much a problem as problematic academics.

Cheerleaders

As a funder, I saw many partnership proposals coming in from academics and communities/users. After a number of mistakes we learned how to spot the fake ones, for example: the proposal didn't provide a name and address for the community contact; there was no money set aside to pay a consultancy fee for individuals who were based in communities and could not be expected to work for free; the academics confused focus groups with real involvement; the community only had the lowly tasks of interviewing – they were not involved from the start and would not be involved in the conclusions/recommendations.

The token individual

Sometimes our projects would have one disabled person, an older person, and someone from a black and minority ethnic (BME) perspective on the team. Sometimes as the funder we tried to encourage an academic proposing the project to add this into their proposal. This was usually a mistake, because if the academic didn't propose it from the start themselves, then they would probably not take it seriously. Often, these token individuals were only appointed after the project had been funded. In most cases, either the token individual ran the risk of being isolated within the team, or their own individual voice became too strong – there was no support for their role in linking back to the community in a way that would allow them to represent perspectives other than their own.

Numbers, power, plans, and meetings

Usually if the academic team says 'thanks so much for your contributions, now we'll go away and make sense of it', you can detect the exact moment when partnership fails. Unless meaning and leadership are negotiated throughout the whole process, then it's fake. There are generally indicators of where the power lies in a research project: the balance of numbers in the room between the researcher and the participants; the involvement of users/communities in setting aims and in planning; the number and nature of meetings. Participation with users/communities is almost always about contested knowledge and contested power. If there isn't an argument – or at least a frank dialogue – about these issues, then that usually means that someone's voice is not being heard.

The 'so what'?

BME older people told us that academics were still asking the same questions they had asked 20 years ago. The answer to these questions, very often, was 'so what?' They were the wrong questions then and they were the wrong questions now. For the academics the partnership was all about producing peer-reviewed articles and journals – but the older people wanted something different. They wanted to see results that the community valued, not simply what academics wanted. People with learning difficulties in a particular town in the English Midlands said that some academic work could be quite useful, but for the most part it didn't really relate to their lives and the changes they wanted to see.

The funder

The funder is often the hidden partner and the hidden power. The funder's priorities often don't reflect what communities actually want, but communities (and their academic allies at times) try to bend their needs to fit in with the funder's priorities. This can be a bad strategy in that it brings funding, but takes away energy and purpose. A group of black women said that, from their own experience, if the funder couldn't adapt to meet their issues then they'd rather not have the money. A group of people with learning difficulties in Lancashire accepted the offer of seed-fund support, but only on condition that they could interview the consultants first.

A user view

There's a brilliant presentation from Jackie Downer (MBE, a campaigner for people with learning disabilities) reflecting on the user experience, which, as a funder, I've used for more than a decade:

- It wasn't an easy road.
- If you don't know it, you don't get the piece of cake.
- Are they (the researchers) *really* ready for us? ... And are we (people with learning difficulties) ready for *them*?
- Why are you doing it?
- Who gets the money?
- Do we (people with learning difficulties) really want it?
- Are you going to make a difference?
- Review what you're doing. Show us the good and the bad.
- Let us get paid.
- Please remember to say 'goodbye' to us.
- We need to be ready as well.
- We need to get the credit too.

Glastonbury and goldfish

It really is like being in a fish tank at times – the proverbial goldfish bowl: stifling. Not fool's gold though – precious academic gold, rare earth research minerals from Formula 1 high-performance minds. And yet at other lotus-petal moments, it's like Glastonbury for genius, innovation, passion, human advancement, compassion, creativity, and light.

So, so many quiet-revolutionaries are wise and content enough to know that all they need do is change or improve even one cog in their portion of the world. Or maybe if they really strike it rich, they might put a new engine in – an engine that runs off recycled dandelion juice and is made from graphene by wholesome local folks on a living wage of £18-ish an hour.

So many once-quite-quirky revolutionaries have been sucked in, like a blue-bottle gets sucked in to those horrid flytraps they have in our ubiquitous kebab shops that frazzle and zap 'em whilst you wait. Sucked into the system, the rigours and rhythms of the predictable, and the march of method that storms right past the magic.

At times it's like you're talking to someone: enthusing, engaging, extrapolating, augmenting, theorizing to potentials – like Tim Leary,[1] high flying – co-creatively … then A Zeus Marimba! I'm struck by an image of my co-creator shrinking, his/her voice getting higher in pitch, lower in volume, disappearing into their own naval – deep, deep inside where the conversation continues alone in the dark for an indeterminate period.

Amongst the many, many bright, playful, fiery-playful, inspiring eyes, you do often come across the ones – you know the ones – the ones that are on backwards, withdrawn behind a Wall Street Stock Exchange-type screen of acronyms, theories, treatises, hypotheses, funding-speak, doctrines, and procedures.

So until five years ago, this whole parallel universe of research with the Arts and Humanities Research Council was, at its quantum metric core essence, a black hole, zero point. And 99.9 per cent of those I have met I have connected with. Still, many feel the pitiless aftertaste of perhaps not having connected at all.

Sometimes it all seems really clear: aims, objectives, purpose, legacy, and the rest. I can't help feeling that if some of the people we aim to serve, assist, empower, knew what was being spent to do very little of the aforementioned, they would either implode or revolt.

I turned up at a big do once – a cynic might term it a back-slapping extravaganza; an optimist or someone educated, a top-drawer networking opportunity. I got myself involved in some round-tabling and came up with a few lyrics about the range of topics we were back-slapping about.

Next thing I knew I was closing the event. Honoured indeed, yet no better fed, then or now generally. No deeper ensconced in innovative long-term projects, learning, growing whilst being of value to others – other 'me's' – some of this is my responsibility, yet not all.

Rules

Our faculty has a strategic partnership with a local community health organization. Located in the community they serve, our community partner is able to identify local needs and propose potential collaborative research projects to be undertaken by Masters and final-year student-researchers.

Despite the acknowledged mutual value of this collaboration, proposals have not been developed. In the main this is due to a policy that students cannot 'consult' with third parties during the proposal development stage of the research, thus preventing essential communication between researcher and stakeholder. This example mirrors the wider difficulties in bridging two different cultures of working.

A PhD? She laughed

Without a host institution and a traditional career trajectory in academia, a lot of my work either goes under the radar or is rendered entirely invisible by the lack of the two things mentioned at the start of this sentence.

Major funding and freelance, collaborative research project successes never seem to join up into a coherent body of work (for the freelancers, that is): they (the projects) are great when they are happening – they engage with a diverse set of people; have aims, objectives, strategy; some of them pay badly or not at all, some pay well; and all of them have a theoretical strand and methodology to them – but once they end I am once more out of work and have to start reinventing the wheel, all over again.

Many of my friends – and I consider them friends and colleagues – who are some of the aforementioned 'traditional academics' have their plates piled so high that when I ask to be paid a freelancer's day rate they baulk. I understand that to a certain degree: they often work in their spare time and do much more than their allotted hours; I have met several academics who do their engagement work in their leisure time. So when I ask to be paid for collaborative work, the divide-and-rule begins.

Since 2002, I have worked as an itinerant practitioner, tutor, and researcher, and as it stands today I am applying for a minimum-wage job in a supermarket. And there's nothing wrong with supermarket working, it's just I thought by now, and with my experience, at least one institution might value my work enough to support it for more than a one-day conference, a two-day summit, or a three-day research seminar.

I plough on but feel more and more that, having straddled the two worlds of academia/research and community/practice (and by default, engagement), both camps are beginning to reject me, when I actually see them as two parts of the same organism (the rejection may be my perception, but it is important to bear witness to the fact that I feel like this).

Although I think I fit into academia, that clearly isn't the reality of the situation. I don't actually think I will ever get any kind of contract or recognized position. I want to be part of an academic team, I want to listen and learn, contribute and participate, facilitate and educate, empower, and emancipate.

I want to work both in and beyond the walls of a university. It seems to me that this isn't an option – not for people like me who lack the two things highlighted in the first sentence of this piece – and it's taken me so long to work this out that I am beginning to suspect that I have rendered myself useless to everyone.

In closing I'd like to share this: last year I went for specialist careers advice at the place where I am researching my part-time PhD. I wanted to discuss the problems I am having finding a home for my work and research. The adviser asked me what I thought it meant 'to be an academic'.

I replied that I thought it was a privileged position of teaching and learning, of influence and power; that an academic is a person with specialist knowledge, both a knowledge-maker and researcher, someone who is part of an inward- and outward-facing team, a person who shares and contributes for the greater good of society, and in return enjoys the benefits of being part of a large edifice and scholarly community. She listened to my response, and then she laughed.

She was well-meaning enough, and it's not with her or any of the brilliant academics (of all sorts) that I've had the pleasure to work with that I am disillusioned. If nothing else, at least I've been able to say this out loud.

I choose not to put my name to this, something I am not comfortable with; however, I worry about the negative effect this honesty could have on my tenuous, non-existent career. I actually think this would make the great starting point for a major inquiry into how we do our research.

Shared ideas

In 2011, I was asked to become an integral part of a new community venture in the west of England. I accepted, as I had been looking to work on a sustainability project that looked at community development.

In the initial meetings with my new colleague he asked me to share with him my experiences around community engagement. The equality of our exchange (or was it a non-exchange?) was based on his having the backing of the local council and interested academic idealists, and my having a connection to community and youth groups that could make full use of the vast building that we had a 'free' reign over. Given these equal stakes, he assured me that we would always make joint decisions.

This lasted for a short time. However, he soon got promoted within his organization and our relationship changed. Now the organization also had to make money from the 'shared ideas'. From then on he took notes of our conversations to his organization and would then inform me of the new decisions they had made.

What are universities for?

In the mid-2000s, a UK government body decided to establish an *Engagement Pioneer* programme across the country. Every university was invited to submit a tender to undertake a programme that would bring about 'culture change' in universities. It would transform the way in which researchers related to those outside academia, particularly in their local communities. Applications were channelled through each university's senior management.

A senior researcher, Dr Agra was herself a pioneer of engagement and of approaches that she had learned to call 'participatory action research'. The prospect of being part of a process to bring these techniques to the heart of her institution was appealing. She contacted Professor Horn, the deputy vice-chancellor (director) of her institution, who was coordinating the application process.

Professor Horn's measure of success was simple: he wanted to be able to walk down a street in a deprived area of the city and to find that, when he asked random passers-by what university research was for, they would have a positive answer.

Working with a range of colleagues both within the university and in a wide variety of organizations beyond, Dr Agra and Professor Horn wrote a proposal that envisaged a transformational programme for the university. They negotiated with another leading university in a neighbouring city to submit a joint proposal.

The proposal from two leading institutions – to change the culture of their research to one of engagement and community participation – flew through the shortlisting process. They appeared to have overcome a generation-old rivalry in order to work together. For the preparation of the final proposal, Professor Horn found funds to buy Dr Agra out from her other responsibilities. She won sponsorship from a mobile phone network, a high-tech giant from Silicon Valley, a city-centre visitor attraction, and local community-based organizations with a rich heritage of undertaking research and practical action on social justice. Together the consortium made a case that was coherent and ambitious. A new vice-chancellor, who proudly proclaimed a vision of a university engaged with its community, declared it as visionary.

The consortium was one of just a handful that were awarded 'engagement pioneer' status, with National Lottery-winning levels of funding to match. Dr Agra took up a role directing the initiative. After a honeymoon period of a few months, she realized that the neoliberal model of the university's business plan was at odds with the principles it had proclaimed in its application. The institution was effectively a global corporation that prioritized two income streams – research and teaching. If being an engagement pioneer could deliver short-term gains in increasing income, then it was embraced. If it could not, it would be tolerated, but nothing more. Six months into the role, Professor Horn retired and Dr Agra acquired a new boss, Professor Stag. He moved the pioneer programme from a central position in the university to its marketing department. There was a six-month consultation about the logo. Community-based organizations were side-lined. A group in the collaborating university who promoted science in local schools complained that they had been promised funds, as they were pioneers too. They had prize-winning talents at promoting science.

After over two years spent either writing the application or supposedly directing the pioneer programme, Dr Agra departed the programme. Acknowledging her case for unfair treatment, the union supported a grievance procedure against Professor Stag. Eventually she received an apology. But a letter had already circulated by email from Professor Stag that made it difficult for her to continue any role in the university. A few months later, despite the best efforts of her union to make her case, she was made redundant.

The final twist was that, during the honeymoon period following the award of pioneer status, the vice-chancellor had supported Dr Agra's proposal to bestow honorary doctorates in civil law to two remarkable social justice activists based in the local community. Their awards were presented the day after Dr Agra had received her apology. Following the award, the two newly honoured doctors of civil law wrote to the vice-chancellor proposing a small initiative to allow communities and academics to work together on a research project that would document knowledge and activism amongst marginalized groups of local people. They never received a reply.

Following four years of generously funded activity, there is still no evidence that the engagement pioneer programmes have modified the increasingly neo-liberal business models of the universities that hosted them in any significant way. It has benefited some academics who were involved. Promotion criteria have been updated. Journal papers have been published and awards bestowed for 'outstanding contributions' to public engagement. But if you walk down a street in any major city today and ask any intelligent and informed person what university research is for, I suspect you will get as many blank stares as you would have before the engagement pioneer scheme began.

Epilogue

Most researchers pride themselves on being critical thinkers. Their attempts – and those of their funders – to collaborate with people outside academic and power elites regularly come up against major obstacles. Some fail spectacularly. Yet admitting failure has become increasingly hard. With job insecurity being the norm in the neoliberal university, people's mortgages and lives are on the line. If the research team cannot notch up their project as a success, they may lose pay and the possibility of future funding. And these researchers are relatively powerful compared to a grassroots-based activist or community group. How can the rest of us have a voice in research when even the researchers are beholden to a system that refuses to admit failure? We hope the chapters that follow help enrich the picture presented here and provide some signposts for the future.

Note

1. Tim Leary was an American psychologist and writer who advocated the exploration of the therapeutic potential of psychedelic drugs under controlled conditions.

CHAPTER 2

Making connections in the 'white-walled labyrinth'

Mayra Guzman, Cedoux Kadima, Grace Lovell, Asha Ali Mohamed, Ros Norton, Yosola Olajoye, Federico Rivas and Alpha Thiam

Abstract

What does democratization of knowledge mean? As a youth-led organization, we want to research our own lives, investigate our own stories, and tell them in our own way. Using participatory action research, we were able to challenge the power of academic institutions, their institutional activities, and their impact on our daily lives. This chapter reflects on our learning from working with academic partners to co-design a programme to create a network of groups of young people in the UK with refugee backgrounds. We describe the experience of people of colour working with white researchers, exploring issues of power, exploitation, tokenism, and trophyism. The chapter provides valuable advice to other community organizations and academic partners who wish to work together.

Keywords: participatory action research, co-design, co-production and democratization of knowledge, tokenism, race, youth

Introduction

This chapter presents our reflections as RefugeeYouth – a youth-led programme for young people of refugee background – on our involvement in the Arts and Humanities Research Council (AHRC) co-design programme. We set out to work with academics to co-design and deliver participatory action research (PAR) processes to create a sustained connection between groups of young people with refugee backgrounds in different parts of the UK. Some of these lessons will be useful to other groups similar to us.

The project started in January 2013, with RefugeeYouth working in partnership with four local youth-led community projects – Humanah in Middlesbrough, Teamwork in Birmingham, Mustaqbal in Harrow, and Leeds Dynamic in Leeds. We worked with our principal investigator (PI), Tom Wakeford, at Coventry University (previously at the University of Edinburgh), and with academic partners at Durham, Bradford and Exeter universities. We initially called the project Seen and Heard when we applied

http://dx.doi.org/10.3362/9781780449395.003

for funding; the name of the project was changed by participants to the Web of Connection, which was a better reflection of what we were setting out to achieve.

Participatory action research – of us, for us, and by us

RefugeeYouth has used PAR for community building since the organization's inception, over 12 years ago. We work with a whole range of young people with refugee backgrounds to generate action that brings about change for self and others. Over the years, young people in RefugeeYouth have established a powerful base by using their collective power to research their own lives and generate knowledge. They have used creative communication methods, such as forum theatre, training, reports/books, films, drama, theatre, and art, to spread the word amongst other young people and community members, and to challenge professionals and policymakers who impact upon their lives. For RefugeeYouth, PAR is our research – of us, for us, and by us, guided by the principles of participatory research, such as those cited by Hall and Kidd (1978: 5) and Hall (1997), set out below:

1. Participatory research involves a whole range of powerless groups of people – the exploited, the poor, the oppressed, and the marginal.
2. Participatory research involves the full and active participation of the community in the entire research process.
3. The subject of the research originates in the community itself and the problem is defined, analysed and solved by the community.
4. The ultimate goal is the radical transformation of social reality and the improvement of the lives of the people themselves. The beneficiaries of the research are the members of the community.
5. The process of participatory research can create a greater awareness in the people of their own resources and mobilize them for self-reliant development.
6. It is a more scientific method of research in that the participation of the community in the research process facilitates a more accurate and authentic analysis of social reality.
7. The researcher is a committed participant and learner in the process of research, i.e. a militant rather than a detached observer.

Challenging power in the 'white-walled labyrinth'

The development of our approach to PAR has been deeply informed by the insightful work of some serious academic writers,[1] and we have on many occasions taken our work into university settings. However, working with the Connected Communities programme – a UK initiative involving several government-funded research councils – was the first time RefugeeYouth had intentionally set out to collaborate and co-design something with people in the academic sector.

Carr and Kemmis suggest that conventional research can be seen as an institutionalized activity, part of a structured system of roles and relationships in universities and other powerful institutions. It is primarily intended – despite the 'rhetoric of disinterest' – to serve the interests of those institutions, what is called a 'political economy of knowledge' (Carr and Kemmis, 1986: 217). Brookfield, quoting black academic Leonard Harris, goes further in describing the academy as a 'white-walled labyrinth, with all paths leading to a white, male, western dominated centre' (Brookfield, 2005: 275).

Almost in contradiction to these institutional norms, RefugeeYouth's primary purpose in working with PAR is to fundamentally challenge the power of such institutions, their institutional activities, and their impact on our daily lives. For us, PAR offers the opportunity to research our own lives, and to investigate our own stories and tell them in our own ways. There was bound to be enormous learning in our attempts to work together with academics on this programme – we needed to investigate, evaluate, and learn from our experiences of working with academic partners.

Framing critical questions

To these ends, a small group of eight key participants from different parts of RefugeeYouth spent a weekend together at the end of April 2015. We examined and re-examined our understanding of PAR; we used a critical eye to interrogate our experiences within the academic sector; and we identified a number of areas of discomfort and critical questions that needed further insight.[2] Amongst our critical questions were: Participatory or colonising? Emancipation or appropriation? Whose ends are being served? Whose interests are being met?

Reflections on the process of co-designing our research proposal and drawing up the submission

Following a Connected Communities Summit in 2012, at which one of the authors was a participant, a team at RefugeeYouth worked to identify the areas upon which a research proposal should focus. The idea for the 'web of connection' came out of our experiences engaging with young people with refugee backgrounds who, because of the UK's dispersal system, found themselves living in the north of England. It seemed wise to try to create a PAR project that would engage some of these young people in investigating and critically examining the key issues that emerged in their lived experiences, and which would generate purposeful actions to bring about change for self and others.

The format for submission was complex and – for most of us – impenetrable. Inevitably, busy people dropped out of the process, leaving two of the team to work with our academic partner to draw up the proposal and make the submission. On reflection, it is no surprise that the two were white and English-speaking, educated to postgraduate level. Yet even so, we had to trust our academic partner – whom we barely knew – to take us through the process and rewrite what had been written by our team in order to meet the submission requirements of the Connected Communities co-design programme.

The submission was successful. However, as so many months had passed since the start of the process, most people in RefugeeYouth were both disconnected and suspicious of it – especially of the institutional 'whiteness' of it all. The original ideas generated within RefugeeYouth were, inevitably, distorted through the long process of preparing the submission. Everyone needed to be reconnected.

All parties came together to explore the proposal and co-design the project. Many had not participated in a PAR project before, and many had not gathered with the RefugeeYouth community before. On reflection, we realized that the process whereby we submitted our plan to the research funder had displaced the co-design process. In many ways, the proposal had been designed before people came to the table to discuss how it could be co-designed!

In addition, for some people, involvement with the academic sector bestowed a certain credibility, a status, that again seemed to distort our processes – often we felt that we could not admit to what we didn't know.[3] Over time it felt that PAR became a 'sound bite' to some of the participants, especially those who were working with RefugeeYouth for the first time.

Our project was clearly too ambitious, especially for the given timescale. Yet we had felt that we needed to be ambitious to meet the programme criteria. In addition, too few people were involved in designing and writing the submission. Although many people in RefugeeYouth are educated to degree level, not all are; and for many, English is a second language – speaking it is one thing, but reading and writing academic texts can be deeply excluding. On reflection, it was too complex a proposal and too many of those involved in its 'delivery' were new to PAR processes.

What did we learn? We frequently experience conventional researchers taking and using (stealing) our stories, using our images to enhance their images, and doing research 'on' us whilst pretending to do research 'with' us. Whilst the Connected Communities programme gave us a chance to propose something different – and our academic partner certainly emerged as one who wanted to learn with us – the submission process required us to jump through conventional hoops. Our attempts to formulate and co-design research of, by, and for the people in RefugeeYouth were severely challenged.

Entering academic spaces

On a number of occasions, we were invited to make presentations at Connected Communities events and festivals. In many ways, these helped a great deal to give our diverse groups a focused way of coming together to learn and to get to know one another. We were able to take time together researching specific issues in our lives, reflecting and extracting knowledge that we wanted to disseminate, and then develop creative strategies for presenting these to the people involved with the programme.

On each occasion, after having worked so hard to prepare, we walked into almost empty spaces, to present to three or four people ... why had we bothered? Walking into these spaces, we found ourselves alone, feeling marginalized, sticking out like sore thumbs, often being much younger than anyone else; and many of us were black – often the only black people in the room. We often wondered why we were there ... to meet Connected Communities programme targets? To perform 'community' for the majority of non-community participants? At the very worst, we felt like performing monkeys, the 'exotic other'. One person described RefugeeYouth as 'bid candy'.

What did we learn? The Connected Communities programme brought us into places and spaces where 'people like us' are rarely active. We need to remember that on entering these spaces we will feel the pressure on us to represent the 'other'. We also need to consider the potential consequences of entering these spaces – we might leave the 'other' behind. These reflections leave us with two dilemmas. Firstly, is it ethically sound for RefugeeYouth to participate? By doing so, does RefugeeYouth buy into the form of trophyism[4] that these discussions highlighted? And secondly, what is our ethical duty, if any, to highlight our experiences to the 'academy', to allow for authentic discussion and learning?

The Connected Communities programme has huge potential to 'make the invisible visible' (Smith and Colin, 2001: 65). However, we have come to believe that different conditions are needed to avoid ourselves being subject to trophyism. And we are left with the ethical dilemma: should we join you? If we do, what happens to those 'others', those whom we leave behind in order to sit at your table?

Writing a paper and the power of words

We were asked to join a group that was producing this book – could we submit a chapter? Those who felt able drafted a 500-word abstract, which was accepted. How to proceed? Every time we write things down it becomes 'a truth'. How can we write about 'others' without doing to them what we feel critical of being done to us? In the end, a small group gathered for the weekend with our academic partner and spent 36 hours reading one chapter, line by line, of an article about action research, as advised by Freire (Shor and Freire, 1987). We kept stopping to understand each line, get out the dictionary, and search for other references, using the article to illuminate our experiences of working together on this programme. This was a deeply moving learning experience for all and resulted in us writing a paper that was initially entitled: 'This paper proposes a process for writing a paper that investigates why the proposed paper was not written'. An edited version of this paper is included in this publication (Pearson et al., 2016).

What did we learn? By reading together, in a safe space, we found a remarkable resonance with each other, and with the content of the paper. The chapter became a magnifying glass through which we gained insights into some of the stumbling blocks experienced in our attempts to work together with PAR in RefugeeYouth. We also learned that, in the right context, we can all read, we can all critique, and we can all write. Bell hooks suggests that 'white scholars are bringing certain baggage with them when they look at black culture, no matter how subtle and sophisticated the formulations' (hooks and West, 1991: 36, quoted in Brookfield, 2005: 280). In many ways we cannot know what that 'baggage' is; we can only feel the power of it, every time we engage. And indeed, power raised its head at every stage of the writing and editing process:

- power of 'whiteness';
- power of language;
- power of non-verbal communication – the looks we get and interpret;
- power in roles and ideas of 'leadership';
- power in voice and representation and whose voice counts and where and by whom;
- power of loss of authenticity in playing the game – in the differences between what we do and what we say we do;
- the power of money, dictating what we can do, and the pressure to follow the money at whatever cost;
- the power of fitting in and playing the game.

Complex though it is, we have learned that we must engage with 'the power' if we are to work together to bring about change for ourselves and others.

Working with our academic partners

In the kind of community-connected programme that we have experienced, there is a danger of each of the two sides objectifying the other. We, the community, are invited to the 'high table of the academy'. This leads to an inescapable power imbalance before we even get started. On the other side, we see people whom we think hold the knowledge and resources. Yet, we also gain the impression, however wrongly, that for many in the academy we are perhaps seen as their road to knowledge and resources. Our most recent experience exemplified this: an evaluator came to talk to us about our experiences on the programme. She brought predetermined questions. She said she had a very limited amount of time. Consequently, every time we strayed into territory unknown to her – but important to us – we felt we were rushed along backwards to fit with her pre-written agenda, deriving, we assume, from her need to complete the work and submit on time the report for which she had been commissioned.

In our principal investigator, we found someone who was willing to apologize, to learn with us, and to walk with us to make the path, to work in mutuality. However much he got it wrong (especially in the early days), he opened doors and accompanied us into spaces and places that, otherwise, we know we would have found very intimidating. It took a while for trust to build, but he was patient and did not take offence when we got it wrong. In essence, he really seemed to share our desire to bring about change, and was open to learning from us, as well as with us.

Looking back, we reflected on how lucky we were when we found academic partners who entered into our community with humility, and who did so as learners whose time and skills in poetry, theatre, and the arts were given freely to enhance our experience.

Some advice to communities (and ourselves)

Carr and Kemmis (1986) advise people in communities that it is 'both legitimate and wise for anyone approached about the possibility of participating in an educational research study to ask whose interests are in fact likely to be served'. They go on to suggest researching the following questions: 'for whom is the research directed?'; 'by whom is it conducted?'; and 'about whom is it written?' (quoted in Brookfield, 2005: 217). Here's what we think can help communities to engage:

Finding academic partners

When your organization is invited to the 'high table', don't let anyone go alone – it needs a few people to suss it out. Go with a critical eye and 'feel' it. When approached by an academic, do as Carr and Kemmis suggest, but also try to find out about the person/people with whom you will need to work. Essentially, you need to feel a sense of shared values and beliefs, some sense of critical awareness. You need to feel their knowledge, understanding, and resistance to the potential for you, as community partners, to be objectified in this process. Explore the potential of partners' motivations at a personal level, not just their knowledge, expertise, and prior experience.

The proposal

Involve key people in the community in drawing up the proposal. Work hard on the 'why'. Whose purposes will it serve? Explore the 'why'. And again … and again! With a strong, clear, shared sense of purpose, it will be much harder for you to get knocked off course in the labyrinth. As you begin to think about how to go about it, we would suggest keeping it small, making it real, and making it doable. Avoid pressure to make it complex and sexy. Use arts and visual methods to make the proposal explicit and owned by everyone, and avoid the pressure to reinterpret this into academic speak. If your academic partner then takes it away and writes it, as they may need to do in order to jump through the conventional hoops, make time for those concerned to read the final proposal 'line-by-line', critically, and together. On this reading, decide collectively: if your proposal is successful – can you all own it?

Power

Acknowledge it, explore it, put it on all your agendas … embed it into your research proposal … give each other permission to examine it … including your academic partners.

Events

Go together – expect discomfort and reflect on this before you go. Be clear about the benefits – to all in the community – in going. What is the minimum you want to get out of it? Can you find a way to present your discomforts? Think about how you can look after each other and if there is action you might take together to avoid being made to feel like the 'sore thumb', or the academics' 'trophies'.

Persistence

'We make the road by walking ...' (Horton and Freire, 1990).[5] Don't give up! There's access to a wealth of people, resources, knowledge, skills, and understandings, all to be gained by being involved. Our web of connection (however fragile) that evolved through the processes described above would not exist otherwise.

Some advice to academics and the academy

Angela Davis (1990: 5) tells us: 'lift as we climb ... in such a way as to guarantee that all of our sisters, regardless of social class, and indeed all of our brothers, climb with us'. We contend that most community organizations, along with many in the academic world, would see this as their mission. If you too share these ends, we suggest the following to our academic partners:

Community engagement

Go to community tables, rather than always inviting them to yours.

Diversity

Break down the 'white-walled labyrinth' – find your sisters and brothers in the academy who have first-hand knowledge and experience of PAR (or related approaches), and involve them from the start in supporting innovative processes of engagement. If they are not there to find inside, move outside.

Submission and co-design – the power of words

To the funders: take the competitive element out of the submission procedure. For communities with a genuine need for research, the co-design process should start with the proposal and submission. So make it part of the process and thus the learning. Recognize that a range of art and visual methodologies can be integral to the co-design process and outcome, i.e. don't expect a conventional proposal/submission, dependent on the language of the academic world.

Power of self

Take a critical, self-reflexive approach to working with communities. Be aware of and investigate the impact of your whiteness, your language, your knowledge. Search for accessible ways to support the people in communities to engage authentically with the wealth of ideas out there, to gain the confidence to do so. Above all, remember we are all researchers, we are all participants – so be humble, be a learner.

Power of institution

Take on board and work with the evaluative feedback that communities are working to give you. Engage with communities who have worked with you to learn how you might support the authentic involvement of communities when inviting them to the 'high table of the academy'! Think about how you might authentically engage with the knowledge of community researchers when planning events. Invite the community to join you in the process of organizing events.

Use some of your resources to support the communities whose members are not formally trained academics to engage in dialogue: perhaps create events that bring the different communities together to share their experiences and learning – or provide the resources for the communities to do that for themselves. Think about the power that could emerge if communities in the research programme were to join forces, and how much learning there would be for the academy in that. Finally, perhaps take the following words and reflect on them critically: emancipatory research requires researchers in universities to 'move beyond [y] our universities and professional associations to build new infrastructure that can facilitate the free exchange of ideas, tools, and people needed for the greater democratization of knowledge' (Ginwright, 2008: 21).

Notes

1. For example, Paulo Freire, Anisur Rahman, Orlando Fals Borda, Myles Horton, Budd Hall, bell hooks, Peter Reason, John Elliot, Angela Davies, Cornell West, Stephen Kemmis, Stephen Brookfield, Michele Fine, Sabo Flores, Ernie Stringer – to mention but a few.
2. In the spirit of PAR, we took our reflections shortly afterwards to a gathering at the Centre for Social Justice and Community Action at Durham University. We had been invited to offer a workshop on RefugeeYouth's ways of working with PAR at the launch of their Participatory Research Hub.
3. Working with a poem from *Knots* by R.D. Laing (1970) was deeply illuminating for us. We cannot reproduce it here for copyright reasons, but it can easily be found by searching online and selecting 'Images'. We were also inspired by *Caminante no hay camino* by Antonio Machado (Libero Pensare, 2013).
4. Trophyism is more than mere tokenism. Tokenism is a policy of formally complying with efforts to achieve a goal by making small, token gestures. We see 'trophyism' as a state of affairs whereby, in this context, you (academics) have got us to the table to serve your purposes, without due consideration of the effect this process might have on us. It is a form of exploitation.
5. Taken, we believe, from the poem by Machado, *Caminante no hay camino*.

References

Brookfield, S.D. (2005) *The Power of Critical Theory for Adult Learning and Teaching*, Open University Press, Maidenhead.

Carr, W. and Kemmis, S. (1986) *Becoming Critical: Education, Knowledge and Action Research*, Deakin University Press, Lewes.

Connected Communities (2014) <https://connected-communities.org> [accessed 4 August 2016].

Davis, A.Y. (1990) *Women, Culture and Politics*, Vintage Books, New York, NY.

Ginwright, S. (2008) 'Collective radical imagination: youth participatory action research and the art of emancipatory knowledge', in J. Cammarota and M. Fine, (eds), *Revolutionizing Education, Youth Participatory Action Research in Motion*, Routledge, New York, NY.

Hall, B.L. (1997) 'Looking Back, Looking Forward: Reflections on the origins of the International Participatory Research Network, and the Participatory Research Group in Toronto, Canada', Paper presented at the Midwest Research to Practice Conference in Adult Continuing Education, Michigan State University, East Lansing, 15–17 October.

Hall, B.L. and Kidd, J.R. (eds) (1978) *Adult Learning: A Design for Action: a Comprehensive International Survey*, Pergamon Press Oxford.

hooks, b. and West, C. (1991) *Breaking Bread: Insurgent Black Intellectual Life*, South End Press, Boston, NY.

Horton, M. and Freire, P. (1990) *We Make the Road by Walking: Conversations on Education and Social Change*, Temple University Press, Philadelphia, PA.

Laing, R.D. (1970) *Knots*, Routledge, London.

Libero Pensare (2013) 'Caminante, no hay camino (Antonio Machado)', <www.liberopensare.com/foto/631-caminante-no-hay-camino-antonio-machado> [accessed 4 August 2016].

Pearson, L., Sanchez Rodriguez, J. and Mohamed, A.A. (2016) 'A puzzling search for authenticity within academia', in People's Knowledge Editorial Collective (eds), *People's Knowledge and Participatory Action Research: Escaping the White-Walled Labyrinth*, pp 63–72, Practical Action Publishing, Rugby <http://dx.doi.org/10.3362/9781780449395.007>.

RefugeeYouth (2016) <http://www.refugeeyouth.org> [accessed 4 August 2016].

Shor, I. and Freire, P. (1987) *A Pedagogy for Liberation: Dialogues on Transforming Education*, Bergin & Garvey, Westport, CT.

Smith, S.E. and Colin III, S.A.J. (2001) 'An invisible presence, silenced voices: African Americans in the adult education professoriate', in V. Sheared and P. Sissel (eds), *Making Space: Merging Theory and Practice in Adult Education*, Bergin & Garvey, Westport, CT.

About the authors

Mayra Guzman, Cedoux Kadima, Grace Lovell, Asha Ali Mohamed, Ros Norton, Federico Rivas and **Alpha Thiam** are current or past members of RefugeeYouth, UK.

CHAPTER 3
Examining our differences

*Asha Ali Mohamed, Asma Istwani, Beatriz Villate,
Emilia Ohberg, Eva Galante, Fatma Mohamed,
Ijaba Ahmed, Hinda Mohamed Smith, Lucy Pearson,
Mayra Guzman, Salma Istwani, Shanti Sakar,
Susanna Hunter-Darch and Tamanna Miah*

Abstract

How can shared spaces inspire and empower us to challenge cultural norms in a wider struggle for social justice? As women from different backgrounds, we explore issues of sexism, sexuality, intersectionality, and identity, uncovering the multiple challenges of race and gender, as we describe the processes of collective critical reflection and writing in setting up a group for girls and women. Our personal accounts highlight the power and value of these shared spaces for open and honest discussion, enabling us to examine our differences and find our commonalities so that we can work together to fight injustices, such as gender inequality.

Keywords: gender, shared spaces, cultural identity, intersectionality, social justice

Introduction

We are a group of women from diverse backgrounds. We originate from many different countries: Somalia, United Kingdom, Sweden, Malaysia, India, Italy, Syria, Iran, Colombia, and Pakistan. Some of us grew up in the UK; some of us came here later in life, alone or with our families to study, or to escape conflict, or to experience a different life. Our group includes mothers, workers, and students.

We are connected through our involvement with the youth/community organization RefugeeYouth. We have all been involved in women's projects at RefugeeYouth (see 'Making connections in the "white-walled labyrinth"', Guzman et al., 2016), but at different stages of an ongoing journey which has taken place over the past eight years. Some of us were involved in setting up the original 'Girls' Group' in 2007. Others were part of the transformation of this group into the more collectively owned 'Women's Worth'. Others were involved in the most recent manifestation of a women-only space: the 'Women's Circle'.

http://dx.doi.org/10.3362/9781780449395.004

Though none of these projects are currently active, the relationships between the women have remained strong and have grown beyond the confines of any project or organization. There is a shared sense of having experienced something very valuable and special in these women's spaces, and so we decided to get together to write something about what we have learned. We draw on our experiences within RefugeeYouth, as well as our very different life experiences as young women, and also our involvement in other projects and organizations – both in women-only spaces and mixed spaces.

We were interested in making sense of our shared experiences and exploring the importance and value of women's spaces in the wider struggle for social justice, as well as the difficulties and challenges in this work. There are many other women who have been part of this journey, but this chapter has been put together by 14 of us. The process of writing collectively has been challenging, especially when working to a deadline. Three of us took on the role of typing and structuring the article, but the themes and ideas were all generated through a day-long workshop where all of us were present. Direct quotes from people at the workshop appear throughout to illustrate the points that we all wanted to convey. These quotes are unattributed and appear in italics. We have also included quotes and ideas from the various articles that we have read to help us make sense of our experiences.

We are aware that a process for exploring and sharing learning that is based around reading and writing is not the most accessible method, and can exclude some people. For this reason we strongly believe that creative means of expression such as art, theatre, film, and music are powerful and important. We present this chapter alongside *Our Journey* – a film which was made by the Women's Circle (2012) and which explores feminism and what it means to be a woman.

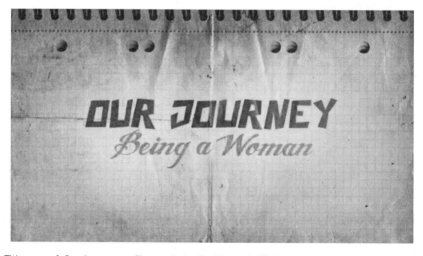

Title page of *Our Journey* – a film made by the Women's Circle

Why do we need women's spaces?

We live in a world where gender inequality exists. There are many issues that we have to contend with as young women in particular. In our society, women are expected to behave in a certain way. We are judged by our appearance above everything else. These expectations are widely perpetuated by the media, music videos, and celebrity culture, usually without critical challenge. There are also different religious and cultural interpretations of how women should behave in society, which can make us feel restricted and oppressed.

> *It seems that as women we are always a reflection of a man's society. We are shaped by society's expectations of us as women. If we gather as women, we can start to break free from these expectations and explore who we are and what we want … be ourselves and try to gain back our identities.*

Some of us have long recognized the need for women's spaces.

> *There was plenty of support and activities for children and young men in our community, but generally, young women were expected to be in the home.*

But some of us didn't immediately understand or accept this need. Some of us come from communities where women are often expected to be separate from men because of cultural and religious traditions.

> *I didn't get it – I used to think "if we want to be in split groups we can go to the mosque".*

In contrast to this, RefugeeYouth has been an open and inclusive community space, which is really valuable to us. Some of us felt as if creating a separate women's space would be going against that inclusive ethos that we held so dear.

> *When it came to Women's Worth that togetherness stopped, and I thought "why are they doing this – there's no problem here between men and women".*

However, through our work, a number of things emerged that highlighted the need for separate women's spaces.

> *When I first experienced RefugeeYouth, I was so blown away by that space, by the energy, and the feeling that it was really open and everyone can just be themselves. But the longer I spent in it, I realized that that wasn't true for everybody and that there were a lot of unspoken tensions.*

We recognized a lack of young women participating in the mixed projects we were involved in. In the mixed spaces, lots of girls came once and never came back again – something wasn't right.

> *Going through the journey of Women's Circle with others, and listening and learning from other women really changed my mind. Most projects are dominated by men, and I realized that some young women wouldn't go into those spaces.*

Mural by members of the Women's Circle

In some of the male-dominated spaces, we often found that young men didn't want to bring their sisters or their girlfriends into them because they felt like these were predatory spaces, and that their sisters and girlfriends wouldn't be respected there. Sometimes it felt like young men only wanted to encourage young women to get involved in order to chat them up and to increase their own chances of getting a girlfriend.

There were also problems encountered with some parents and communities not allowing young women to participate in mixed projects.

> When we started our project, we had to sit down with the parents and explain to them why the project was mixed, because they thought it was like a dating club … They did change though, and as trust was built, some of the parents became really supportive of the work.

We realized that there is a lot of work that needs to be done with young women and parents to enable them to participate in mixed spaces. We recognize the importance of working with the families and the communities to develop trust and understanding, instead of just saying 'they are wrong'.

We also found that the majority of youth projects are run in the evenings, which sometimes poses an additional barrier to getting younger women involved.

> It was hard for me to convince my parents to let me come to the workshops – that was quite difficult for me.

In addition, we came to realize the needs of young mothers in our network – especially those who were here in the UK without partners, family, or community support networks, and who were often very isolated and unable to participate in most 'youth' spaces.

In our experience, youth projects specifically aimed at young women often offer basic service provision focused around stereotypical 'girls' activities', such as hair, make-up, and jewellery. In contrast to this, we aspire to create a space in which women can critically explore gender issues in a social and political context. We want to be able to come together to understand and challenge the sexism embedded in our society, and to have space to explore the issues that women face, in particular young women from refugee and migrant backgrounds.

We don't want to have to justify our experiences to men, but instead we want to have space to explore them in an accepting, supportive environment of sisterhood.

> In society it feels like we don't really have women's spaces where we can "be".

Sisterhood – finding our commonality

There is a power and a value to being together with other women who are all so different – we all come from different backgrounds, experiences, countries, and cultures, and that doesn't happen very often. Sometimes people assume that in a women-only space we do our hair and our nails and get angry about men. But it's more than that. We really value having a space to be together as women.

> Being with just women feels like it's automatically a safe space.

> As a woman, it's important to be comfortable amongst women; having a space where we can be and share with other women.

We look back on the Women's Circle as a special, powerful, and unique space. Our experiences of bringing women together through residentials and arts events created a safe environment where people could be their true selves.

> The group was what was needed in my life at that time. I found a space which is non-judgemental and where people are open to exploring what feminism is.

> It's amazing how such a comfortable, strong, solid group was built in such a short time – it's really unique.

> We worked together so well, in a way that I've never really experienced with a group. I felt so comfortable straight away – in a way that I don't feel even with some members of my family, or some friends that I have known for years.

For a women's space to be valuable it needs to be open, inclusive, welcoming, and non-judgemental; a space where you can turn up and be confused, where it's okay to say 'I don't know'.

> *I tried to get involved in other activist groups, and I felt like I wasn't good enough for them, because I didn't have the textbook speak behind what I was thinking or what I was feeling.*

> *Here, you throw an idea out to the group: you might know a little bit, then someone else might know more than you, and they teach you, but without making you feel small ... It's like we all know bits and pieces and we put it together in a puzzle ... it's about learning and growing.*

Together we feel safe and comfortable to explore issues that don't get explored in other spaces. We explore and discover things ourselves. This is important in terms of ownership over our work and our own thoughts.

> *We don't victimize ourselves, but we know there are issues we need to talk about. But it comes from within – no one is telling us we are oppressed.*

> *Discussions around subjects like arranged marriage and sexual health I found really useful, because I didn't have another space to talk to people about these things.*

Sexism is not always acknowledged. A lot of people think it doesn't exist anymore, or that women overreact. The American author and feminist bell hooks wrote:

> As all advocates of feminist politics know, most people do not understand sexism or if they do they think it is not a problem. Masses of people think that feminism is always and only about women seeking to be equal to men. And a huge majority of these folks think feminism is anti-male. Their misunderstanding of feminist politics reflects the reality that most folks learn about feminism from patriarchal mass media. (hooks, 2000: 1)

For Baxter and Cosslett (2015: 289), the problem is no less current: 'The idea that feminism is obsolete is one of the most dangerous myths being bandied around at the moment.'

Our own experiences seem to support the view that sexism still exists.

> *It's nice to have an environment where you don't have to justify yourself, where you can share your experiences and people accept them and don't think you are overreacting.*

Coming together as women we gain awareness of the issues affecting us so that we can be stronger and can start to challenge and change the way things are.

> *Exploring our experiences as women together arms us so that when we go back into the world we are more sure of ourselves.*

As bell hooks reminds us:

> Feminist sisterhood is rooted in shared commitment to struggle against patriarchal injustice, no matter the form that injustice takes. Political

solidarity between women always undermines sexism and sets the stage for the overthrow of patriarchy (hooks, 2000: 15).

Intersectionality – examining our differences

We cannot claim that merely bringing women together helps solve society's problems – it's not as simple as that. Because we are not just women; we are many different things. Our identities are multiple and complex. We come from different cultural contexts. Some of us are mothers. We have different skin colours, different sexualities, different social classes. We have different backgrounds, different experiences, and different lives.

Intersectionality is a word used to describe:

> the complex, irreducible, varied, and variable effects which ensue when multiple axes of differentiation – economic, political, cultural, psychic, subjective, and experiential – intersect in historically specific contexts. The concept emphasises that different dimensions of social life cannot be separated out into discrete and pure strands (Brah and Phoenix, 2004: 76).

It's complicated. Our experiences as women take place within the wider context of all the other aspects of who we are. When we experience multiple forms of oppression it can sometimes be hard to make sense of this.

> *I get very confused because I don't only think about my gender but also my sexuality as a lesbian; if a man challenges me is it about my gender or my sexuality?*

Our differences mean that we have different relationships with the concept of feminism. For many of us, we didn't automatically see ourselves as feminists; in fact we felt quite distanced from the world of feminism, which many of us see as a white woman's domain. 'It seems to me that the word feminist, and the idea of feminism itself, is also limited by stereotypes' (Ngozi Adichie, 2014: 3).

> *Every time I think about feminists I think about white academics, and that I need to speak and behave a certain way in order to be part of the group. I have also known this in all the community settings I have worked in; it's always the white middle-class woman saying how things should be done.*

> *If you are white middle class you can be whatever you want, but if you are ethnic this or that your culture may not allow it, it's difficult.*

Writing about her relationship with feminism, Nigerian author Chimamanda Ngozi Adichie recalls being told by a Nigerian academic woman 'that feminism was not our culture, that feminism was un-African' (2014: 10). We feel that the dominant narrative voice in feminism is the voice of the privileged white woman, often seeking to liberate 'oppressed ethnic minority women'. It is very important to us to move away from this.

I'm always aware of how, as ethnic minority women, we are seen as oppressed, and it feels like there is one dominant feminist voice which we are supposed to listen to.

Black and Asian women are doing feminism but at times they don't know they are doing it, in Africa they just do it! African women just do it and they don't have a label for feminism, they have been doing it for a long time but they don't write about it and give it fancy words.

People like us don't have space to talk and write and be listened to. Just because you can't write a certain way doesn't mean you shouldn't be listened to.

Perhaps feminism is something only white middle-class women can afford to do? Historically, it can be argued that working-class women don't have the time or the money to be feminist activists because they are busy looking after the kids or working to earn money. Could it be that we only associate white middle-class women with feminism because they have had more opportunity to occupy that space and dominate the narrative?

The media and academics alike can use words like 'feminist' so that they can distance themselves, in order to label people and make people feel less able to engage and own the knowledge that they have. In the Women's Circle we have explored the different ways in which you can be a feminist, and we go into this in more depth in the film *Our Journey*. We have learned that there are different ways in which we can enact our feminist values.

It made me realize that to be a feminist you don't have to shave your head or wear no make-up.

In the Women's Circle I was challenged in a completely different way. Things came back that I thought I had made my mind up about years ago, and I was forced to reassess.

As soon as you start to defend your rights, you become a feminist.

It's important that whilst exploring our experiences of oppression as women, we also unpack our various privileges, and enter into honest, open dialogue about our differing race, class, and sexuality, and how this impacts on our relationships with one another as women. This is something we recognize we need to do more of – it's part of an ongoing journey.

I'm so grateful to you guys for helping me to understand what it means to be white. If I'd never come into this environment I probably wouldn't even be aware of my whiteness or what that means in any sense.

We also need to explore and look at class within this context and historical events where white women have oppressed black women, such as during slavery times and South African apartheid.

It feels to us that black women cannot avoid awareness of their race, whilst white women are rarely forced to confront and explore their whiteness. There need to be more spaces for this to happen amongst white women, if we are to try and build a genuine and honest sisterhood which is not undermined by our racial differences. Because 'as long as women are using class or race power to dominate other women, feminist sisterhood cannot be fully realized' (hooks, 2000: 16). This sense of feminism needing to involve all women is shared by Barbara Smith (2014: 39):

> Feminism is the political theory and practice that struggles to free all women: women of colour, working-class women, poor women, disabled women, lesbians, old women, as well as white, economically privileged heterosexual women. Anything less than this vision of total freedom is not feminist, but merely female self-aggrandisement.

We take an important lesson from the history of feminist struggle, reminded once again by bell hooks (2000: 15): 'Sisterhood could never have been possible across the boundaries of race and class if individual women had not been willing to divest of their power to dominate and exploit subordinated groups of women.'

Internalized sexism

As women we can also oppress ourselves and each other without any input from men. We often have stereotypical views of each other. In fact, those who are most judgemental about the way women look, act, and dress are often other women. We need to try and move beyond that, and not make judgements about each other based on appearances and assumptions. bell hooks talks about 'the enemy within' in reference to ways of thinking amongst women that compound our oppression (2000: 14): 'we had been socialized by patriarchal thinking to see ourselves as inferior to men, to see ourselves as always and only in competition with one another for patriarchal approval, to look upon each other with jealousy, fear and hatred.'

Some young women who got involved in the Women's Circle were never seen without make-up. Sometimes it feels like make-up is used as a form of protection. When some of these young women finally took off their make-up in front of their peers, it felt like a big step.

> *To create an environment where people can feel safe enough to take off their make-up is really amazing.*

However, it's important that women always have choice. We don't feel in any position to pressure other women to dress or act in a certain way. When the time is right people may feel comfortable to take off their make-up, or take off their headscarf, but it's about giving people the freedom to arrive at these decisions by themselves, and accepting women as they are and how they want to be.

We need to be open to all different types of women, and be prepared to be challenged. There are so many different types of women in the world. Just because we are women, it doesn't necessarily mean we have anything else in common. It takes time and work to discover our commonality. Shared experiences help us to connect.

We were intrigued by each other, by each other's stories and backgrounds.

Working together to challenge sexism

We find ourselves constantly fighting to justify why a women-only space is needed. We often struggle to articulate this in a way that men can understand and accept.

There's a difference between having separate spaces and being separatist.

We are on a journey to fight for equality and social justice for all. We do not want to be separate from men, but recognize that within this journey there are different needs and types of injustice and oppression, which need to be addressed in different ways.

We recognize that different spaces and projects are needed in order for different people to be able to participate, according to where they are at in their lives at the time. It is within this context that we strongly advocate the need for separate women's spaces. 'We didn't bond against men, we bonded to protect our interests as women.' (hooks, 2000: 15)

However, we recognize that there is no sense in only addressing the issue of sexism amongst women.

We need moments to gather our ideas and share our experiences … but we also need that moment of confrontation.

Women suffer from living in a sexist world, but men also suffer from the gender expectations ingrained in our society. Sexism affects boys and girls, as society dictates how we should act and behave. We see this evidenced by all the 'boy's behaviour courses' that take place in children's centres as well as having specialists in schools to work with boys. Instead of children being encouraged to explore and experiment and find out who they want to be, gender-specific roles and stereotypes are forced on boys and girls from a very young age.

I was walking in the street and I saw a two-year-old boy crying and his carer (a woman) was screaming at him and telling him "boys don't cry".

In her book *We Should All be Feminists*, Ngozi Adichie (2014: 26) talks about the dangers of prescribing gender stereotypes on boys: 'We do a great disservice to boys in how we raise them. We stifle the humanity of boys. We define masculinity in a very narrow way. Masculinity is a hard, small cage, and we put boys inside this cage.'

If men can also break the rules of what is expected of them, then perhaps we can start to change things together.

How can we change our roles in society if men don't also change their roles?

In order to really challenge sexism and sexist behaviour, women and men need to be on the same page. But we have lots of questions about how and where this conversation should start:

- When it's recognized that male sexism needs to be challenged, whose responsibility is it to challenge it?
- Is it women's role to challenge men?
- Will men recognize that it's happening if we don't?
- How do you get people to understand that sexism exists?

We recognize some important parallels between racism and sexism. Just like racism, sexism is often unconscious and unintended. Just as when unconscious racism is pointed out, men's first reaction when their sexism is pointed out is to be hurt and defensive.

> *If I need that support [of the Women's Circle] to develop that awareness and explore that, maybe it's the case that men also need support to develop awareness of their maleness and their sexism. They don't necessarily know about it … because they are part of the dominant power, and they are not suffering the consequences of sexism.*

Ngozi Adichie identifies the problem that 'many men do not actively think about gender or notice gender' (2014: 42). From our experience, we have seen that when it's just women challenging men, then it turns into a battle, and men will become defensive. If the process is led only by women, then it tends to create animosity.

Some men feel threatened by the idea of feminism. This comes, I think, from the insecurity triggered by how boys are brought up, how their sense of self-worth is diminished if they are not 'naturally' in charge as men. (Ngozi Adichie, 2014: 42)

We need to build an environment where both women and men think about and challenge these things. We need men to avoid going on the defensive, but instead to recognize that we live in a sexist world, and that as men and women we all unconsciously enact sexist behaviour. As Baxter and Cosslett (2015: 287) put it:

> We need to realize that patriarchy … in other words, the status quo where men run the world and women run their households – is bad for men too, because it limits who they can be as people and as sexual beings. But most of all, we need to confront those people who still claim that we don't live in a man's world, and that we don't need feminism anymore, and we need to laugh them right out of the fucking park.

We all need to develop this awareness and challenge ourselves and each other, and also be open to being challenged without seeing it as a personal affront. We want to find our brothers who are already engaged in anti-sexism work, and work with them to figure out a way forward.

I do think we need a separate space because there are times when we can't discuss some issues with men around because they will jump on the issues and dominate the conversation … but we also need the space to come together to discuss these issues. We need to be careful we don't create a bubble where everyone feels strong and supported within the group, and when they leave the group society hits them in the face because sexism exists in the world.

Together we are powerful and, when we are ready, we want to engage men in this continuing dialogue to bring about greater change.

References

Baxter, H. and Cosslett, R.L. (2015) *The Vagenda*, Vintage Random House, London.

Brah, A. and Phoenix, A. (2004) 'Ain't I a woman? Revisiting intersectionality', *Journal of International Women's Studies*, 5: 75–86.

Guzman, M., Kadima, C., Lovell, G., Mohamed, A.A., Norton, R., Rivas, F. and Thiam, A. (2016) 'Making connections in the "white-walled labyrinth"', in People's Knowledge Editorial Collective (eds), *People's Knowledge and Participatory Action Research: Escaping the White-Walled Labyrinth*, pp. 23–32, Practical Action Publishing, Rugby <http://dx.doi.org/10.3362/9781780449395.003>.

hooks, b. (2000) *Feminism Is For Everybody – Passionate Politics*, SouthEnd Press, Cambridge, MA.

Ngozi Adichie, C. (2014) *We Should All Be Feminists*, Harper Collins, London.

Smith, B. (2014) 'Racism and women's studies', in P.R. Grzanka (ed.), *Intersectionality: A Foundations and Frontiers Reader*, pp. 38–41, Westview Press, Philadelphia, PA.

Women's Circle (2012) *Our Journey – Being a Woman* <https://vimeo.com/64554574> [accessed 5 August 2016].

About the authors

Asha Ali Mohamed, Asma Istwani, Beatriz Villate, Emilia Ohberg, Eva Galante, Fatma Mohamed, Ijaba Ahmed, Hinda Mohamed Smith, Lucy Pearson, Mayra Guzman, Salma Istwani, Shanti Sakar, Susanna Hunter-Darch, and **Tamanna Miah** are members of the Women's Circle.

CHAPTER 4

Cultivating an anti-racist position in post-race society

Jasber Singh

Abstract

Why does the practice of action research for social change require a critical engagement with issues of race, power, and identity? How do we cultivate an anti-racist and post-colonial position when carrying out action research? Through a brief description of my experience of racism and imperialism from a personal and professional standpoint, I explore three overlapping ideas. Firstly, recognizing the dominant position of racism in our culture; secondly, recognizing race as an experience; and thirdly, recognizing the need for an ongoing process of 'decolonizing' our thinking. The current post-race society denies the existence of racism, yet has seen racism perpetuated and embedded in institutions. I offer suggestions for how we might cultivate an anti-racist perspective to avoid the pitfalls and dangers of this post-race thinking.

Keywords: action research, social justice, racism, essentialism, decolonization, post-race society

Introduction

Growing up in Britain, I was regularly taken to visit my extended family who lived in the Global South (see Glossary). This experience made me aware of the impact of racism and imperialism in both settings and their horrific effects (Virdee, 2014). Later I was inspired by resistance to injustice, such as the anti-racism movement in the UK. In this chapter, I have combined theory, reflections from practice, and my lived experiences of racism, alongside learning from the anti-racist movement (e.g. Hall, 1978).

I started to do what most formally trained academics would call 'action research' (see Glossary) when I was a youth worker in Lancashire in the north of England. My experiences have led me to conclude that cultivating an anti-racist position is important for action research practice. In this chapter, I will focus on cultivating an anti-racist position, rather than exploring the racial discourse around action research, which has been done elsewhere (Johns, 2008; Foldy, 2015).

It is difficult to cultivate an anti-racist position in a society that denies the existence of racism. One concept that helps us to understand why so much racism still exists, yet is denied, is that of a 'post-race society'.

http://dx.doi.org/10.3362/9781780449395.005

Racism and the post-race society

Many commentators have reported that we live in an age that is beyond race – a post-race society (Sian et al., 2013). How we arrived at this point can be explained historically. Hesse (2011) has written about three different horizons that can be used to understand and characterize different stages of racism.

The 'racist' horizon

This is a period of overt racism, based on false science that described race as biologically determined. The hierarchy of race was linked to the justification of slavery and colonialism. Slave rebellions, anti-colonial struggles, as well as civil rights movements in the West rejected these explicitly racist ideas. In the 1930s and 1940s, major Western powers condemned racism and rejected Nazism and fascist ideologies, despite clinging on to colonies (Hesse, 2011; Sayyid, 2010). Following the rejection of Nazi-inspired scientific assertions, many scientists working alongside the United Nations disputed the idea that race was biologically determined. Overt racism started to recede.

The 'anti-racist' horizon

This describes the period from the 1970s to the 1990s. In this period, anti-racist struggles forced some governments, such as the UK and the USA, to condemn abject racism. For example, rampant racist violence and police denial and oppression, or compulsory virginity tests for South Asian women on arrival in the UK to prove that they were not already married, were directly challenged by anti-racists. Racism constructed through the state was marginalized. However, inequalities and power imbalances were still linked to race and gender.

The 'post-race' horizon

This is the one we are in at the time of writing, and is characterized by the idea that racism is over. The apartheid system in South Africa has gone, Mandela is celebrated as a global statesman, Obama was elected to power for a second term, and there is better representation of non-white people in public life.

The post-race society gives an impression that the dominant white power structures are being challenged. In the words of Sayyid (2010: 3):

> The post-racial is announced explicitly or implicitly by reference to a new cultural disposition in which the representation of people of colour is seen as transforming the whiteness ... associated with Europeans. The splash of colour becomes a metaphor for a landscape no longer polluted by the horrors of racism.

The coming of the post-race society in the UK has been accompanied by cuts to funding for equality initiatives across the country. Unlike housing, health, and welfare payments, equality initiatives are not seen as essential. At the heart of the post-racial argument is the assumption that the era when the British state celebrated every kind of ethno-cultural diversity, and actively opposed racism, is behind us. The post-race society is perpetuated by policymakers who argue, or merely assume, that the policies and legislation currently in place around race equality are good enough to tackle discrimination. If racism is found, these policymakers choose to believe that it is in the minds of a few rogue individuals, rather than being a structural feature of organizations (Farmer et al., 2006).

Many activists and anti-racist scholars wish to reverse the UK's decline into a post-racial society. They argue that racism remains embedded within society through its structures. The long campaign for justice for Stephen Lawrence, for example, exposed institutional racism in the UK police force (Macpherson, 1999; Wikipedia, 2016). The rise of 'stop and search', black deaths in police custody, the 'prevent agenda' that unfairly discriminates against Muslims, the rise of the far right in the form of the English Defence League, British National Party, Britain First, South East Alliance, Fans and Firms against Islam, and the UK Independence Party, alongside widespread Islamophobia, and the UK Government's recent 'go home' campaign on immigration, demonstrate the embeddedness of racism. The Brexit climate in the UK has also shown how the embedded nature of racism surfaces corrosively, with an extraordinary rise in racist attacks and violence in every aspect of British society – from schools, the workplace, and public transport, to the streets. Anti-racist activists and scholars seem to make a compelling argument: race still matters.

Racism and research

Doing action research requires critical engagement with the histories of former colonies and anti-racist struggles in the colonizer nations (Tuhiwai Smith, 2012; Kapoor and Choudry, 2010). Many scholars have critiqued research from an anti-racist and feminist standpoint because women and people of colour are often disempowered by it. Historically, conventional social research was used to strengthen colonial structures in attempts to subjugate, classify, and narrate the 'other'. Anthropological research, in its attempt to understand 'other' cultures, both past and present, tends to reproduce essentialist (see Glossary) views, like the exotic 'other' read through and narrated by a European framework (Spivak and Harasym, 1990). Our awareness of the power of the European to narrate the 'other' from its perspective is crucial. Edward Said describes this as 'orientalism' – an ideological discourse based upon a power/knowledge relationship denying the voice of the other or subaltern (see Glossary) and privileging the European (Said, 1977).

Bhambra (2014) has shown that the systematic exclusion and segregation of African-American sociologists until the 1960s served to promote 'white sociology' by segregating 'black sociology'. Many African-American sociologists have shown that the history of enslavement and colonial domination continues to inform contemporary understandings of sociology (Connell, 2007). This logic could also extend to our understanding of action research in the

UK. Consequently, doing action research without critically engaging with the ideas of a post-race society is likely to reinforce racist and colonial positions.

Responding to the challenges of the post-race society

I have argued that despite the claims made by post-race advocates, racism is ever present. I have also suggested that much conventional research reflects the UK's history of racism and segregation. Considering these points, I will now argue that it is vital to cultivate an anti-racist position and this can be done in three overlapping and continual steps: a) recognizing racism; b) recognizing race as an experience; and c) decolonizing our thinking.

Recognizing racism

The post-racial age, with 'splashes of colour' being represented in key areas of public life, gives the impression that white neocolonial dominance is over. Rather than signify the end of racism, Sayyid (2010: 6) has stated that 'the post-racial society arises not through the elimination of racism, but through a discursive reconfiguration which makes it increasingly difficult to locate racism in western societies except historically or exceptionally'.

Before doing action research, it is important to recognize racism and to start talking seriously about it as a significant issue, especially in a post-racial landscape that seeks to deny its very existence (Sian et al., 2013). Expanding our conversations to explore the ideas underpinning racism, such as white privilege and neocolonialism, can help us develop our collective, politically conscious anti-racist stance.

Recognizing race as experience

How do we ensure that action research takes an anti-racist and post-colonial position? On a basic level, the answer is simple: it has to be framed and conducted in an anti-racist way, so that racism is put at the foreground rather than being denied.

It is difficult, however, to put this into practice. To achieve this requires a critical reflection on how racism has affected our thinking and our being: we need to think ontologically; that is, to think about our experiences of being human. Sayyid (2010: 6) has stated that in the post-race society, 'racism has been reconfigured through the abandonment of "race" as an explicit ontology of the social'. In other words, if the experience of race is denied, then so is the experience of racism. Critically, this indicates that if there is discussion about society which allows for the abandonment of race, white narratives will dominate. Such discussion would strengthen the idea that we live in a post-race society. To counter this dominant narrative requires centring experiences of race and racism, which in turn undermines the post-race society.

Decolonizing our minds

Moving away from post-race ideas requires engaging with racism and decolonizing our thinking and the positions we hold. In *The Post-Colonial Critique*, Spivak and Harasym (1990: 121) write: 'What we are asking for is that the hegemonic [i.e. dominant] discourses, and the holders of the hegemonic discourse, should dehegemonize their position and themselves and learn how to occupy the subject position of the other.'

With this in mind, I ask whether I am doing this rigorously as an action researcher. And more importantly, how would I do this? In *Black Skin, White Masks* (1952), Frantz Fanon showed how the majority of us in the West have imbued colonial thinking through the language we use and education we have attained. His seminal work highlights how difficult it is to decolonize ourselves, as we cannot easily erase the colonial influences from our minds. In spite of the challenge, decolonizing our thinking or at least disrupting a colonial mindset is a crucial part in the 'doing' of action research.

Reflections from practice

For a youth work project, I secured funds that stipulated that the black and Asian young men I worked with were to make a film about what the funders called 'multiculturalism'. The funders wanted to see multicultural Britain through the eyes of these 'other' young men. They had good intentions – the voice of minorities in the town was well-hidden and these resources were aimed at redressing that, to celebrate cultural diversity in the post-race society.

The way the funding was framed made me feel uncomfortable. It trapped minority groups into telling a story from a multicultural perspective. The framing effectively essentialized them. I started to think about how I could approach the work in an anti-racist way whilst using action research. Anti-racist discourse suggests that I had to reframe the questions to avoid entrapping the young men within a culturalist lens. In other words, I did not want them to be trapped in purely 'ethnic' or 'religious' frameworks. I was confident that if the young men decided what the film was about and narrated it in the way they wanted, their minoritized perspective would come through, as their identity shapes how they experience the world.

We started an action research process to make the film. We organized a number of workshops to think through what their story was about. They wanted to make a film about boredom and the subculture around that. The finished film, *The Longest Day* (unpublished), highlighted how there was nothing to do and the days, as a result, felt long.

In the workshops we watched films to inspire our creativity. After watching *Boyz n the Hood*, the 1991 film written and directed by John Singleton, I organized a group discussion to find out what we had learned and how we could apply this knowledge to the film that we were making. One of the young men explained how the film represented black young men in Los Angeles in neither a negative nor positive way, but rather it told their story. We discussed how many films and programmes on TV depicted black or Asian young men in a negative way – the violent gang member, the terrorist, and so on. The members of the youth group were adamant that their film would not draw upon these stereotypes or reinforce essentialist positions, but would narrate their life through their eyes – both positive and negative – as Singleton had also aimed to do. The young men discussed their ideas with passion, composed a storyboard, and made the film. They made a film that subtly resisted adopting the dominant perspective of black and Asian culture. It also showed how the young men faced racism in their everyday life – being followed by security guards and cameras, and being subjected to verbal racism.

Action research within a youth-work setting has to deal with contradictions. For example, providing space to celebrate marginalized cultures, whilst being aware of funders who can tend towards essentializing people through cultural lenses and making trophies of them (see 'Making connections in the "white-walled labyrinth"', Guzman et al., 2016). It also has to be framed in an open way so that people can talk about lived realities. But this open framing should not be so open that it quietly accepts the post-race society position where racism is denied. These complicated ideas, in situ, often feel like a fine line, and the tensions are not so easy to tease out when working with the pressure of deadlines.

In my experience, there are moments when anti-racism starts to matter. Knowing when those moments occur seems more like a 'feeling' – an art – rather than a science (see 'The original citizen scientists', People's Knowledge Editorial Collective, 2016). In the contemporary context, ethnically marked communities continue to be monitored, considered abnormal or 'other', attacked, criminalized, denied services, and to experience poorer life chances. Action research needs to find a way to accommodate that reality rather than deny it. The first step towards this is to cultivate an anti-racist position.

Conclusion

The view that we live in a post-race society is widespread in Europe and North America. Under this view, racism only happens inside the minds of a few peripheral people. It ignores the structural nature of racism in our society. This post-racial perspective presents a serious and daunting challenge because it traps societies in a discourse that assumes overt racism is a thing of the past. The prominence of these claims and assumptions makes ongoing racism even harder to locate and challenge than in previous decades. It becomes important to cultivate an anti-racist position and embrace the spirit of resistance before or whilst doing action research. Furthermore, taking an anti-racist position opens up a conceptual space to broaden the political horizon to include the intersections between gender, class, sexuality, age, disability, and literacy.

This chapter has explored the importance of cultivating anti-racism as an individual position. This approach has its limitations, as it leaves the structural nature of racism largely untouched. Structurally, race and gender and many other ways of knowing have been excluded from the centres of power in Europe, and this has stifled knowledge production. One way to approach this structural problem is to extend anti-racist efforts to the epistemological realm so that different ways of being, imagination, and knowing counter Eurocentric coloniality.

I would like to see the spirit of resistance go on to build collectivity amongst action researchers so that they come together and take part in critical discussion around anti-racism. Through discussion, thinking, innovative theory, and creative practice, we can start to challenge ourselves and imagine a collective anti-racist world, rather than silently allow the post-racial to gain momentum.

References

Bhambra, G.K. (2014) 'A sociological dilemma: race, segregation and US sociology', *Current Sociology* 62: 472 <http://dx.doi.org/10.1177/0011392114524506>.

Connell, R. (2007) *Southern Theory: The Global Dynamics of Knowledge in Social Science*, Allen & Unwin, Crows Nest.

Fanon, F. (1952) *Black Skin, White Masks*, Grove Press, New York, NY.

Farmer, P.E., Nizeye, B., Stulac, S. and Keshavjee, S. (2006) 'Structural violence and clinical medicine', *PLoS Med* 3(10): e449 <http://dx.doi.org/10.1371/journal.pmed.0030449>.

Foldy, E.G. (2015) 'The location of race in action research', in H. Bradbury (ed.), *The SAGE Handbook of Action Research*, 3rd edn, Sage Publications, Chicago, IL.

Guzman, M., Kadima, C., Lovell, G., Mohamed, A.A., Norton, R., Rivas, F. and Thiam, A. (2016) 'Making connections in the "white-walled labyrinth"', in People's Knowledge Editorial Collective (eds), *People's Knowledge and Participatory Action Research: Escaping the White-Walled Labyrinth*, pp. 23–32, Practical Action Publishing, Rugby <http://dx.doi.org/10.3362/9781780449395.003>.

Hall, S. (1978) *Policing the Crisis: Mugging, the State and Law and Order*, Macmillan, London.

Hesse, B. (2011) 'Self-fulfilling prophecy: the post-racial horizon', *South Atlantic Quarterly* 110: 155–78.

Johns, T. (2008) 'Learning to love our black selves: healing from internalized oppressions', in P. Reason and H. Bradbury (eds), *The SAGE Handbook of Action Research*, 2nd edn, Sage Publications, Chicago, IL.

Kapoor, D. and Choudry, A. (eds) (2010) *Learning From the Ground Up: Global Perspectives on Social Movements and Knowledge Production*, Palgrave Macmillan, Chicago, IL.

Macpherson, W. (1999) *The Stephen Lawrence Inquiry*, [online] Report presented to Parliament by the Secretary of State for the Home Department by the Command of Her Majesty, <www.gov.uk/government/uploads/system/uploads/attachment_data/file/277111/4262.pdf> [accessed 5 August 2016].

People's Knowledge Editorial Collective (2016) 'The original citizen scientists', in People's Knowledge Editorial Collective (eds), *People's Knowledge and Participatory Action Research: Escaping the White-Walled Labyrinth*, pp. 103–112, Practical Action Publishing, Rugby <http://dx.doi.org/10.3362/9781780449395.011 >.

Said, E. (1977) *Orientalism*, Penguin, Harmondsworth.

Sayyid, S. (2010) 'Do post-racials dream of white sheep?' Centre for Ethnicity and Racism Study, <http://www.ces.uc.pt/projectos/tolerace/media/Working%20Paper%201/6%20CERS%20-%20Do%20Post-Racials%20Dream%20of%20White%20Sheep.pdf> [accessed 5 August 2016].

Sian, K., Sayyid, S. and Law, I. (2013) *Racism, Governance and Public Policy: Beyond Human Rights*, Routledge, New York, NY.

Singleton, J. (dir.) (1991) *Boyz n the Hood*, Columbia Pictures, USA.

Spivak, G. and Harasym, S. (1990) *The Post-Colonial Critic: Interviews, Strategies, Dialogues*, Routledge, London.

Tuhiwai Smith, L. (2012) *Decolonizing Methodologies: Research and Indigenous Peoples*, 2nd edn, Zed Books, London.

Virdee, S. (2014) *Racism, Class and the Racialized Outsider*, Palgrave Macmillan, London.

Wikipedia (2016) 'Murder of Stephen Lawrence' <https://en.wikipedia.org/wiki/Murder_of_Stephen_Lawrence> [accessed 5 August 2016].

About the author

Jasber Singh works at the Greenwich Inclusion Project, UK.

CHAPTER 5
Poems

ChriS JaM

Abstract

Poetry is used here as a means of communicating complex ideas that have arisen during the collaborative research processes in the course of co-producing this book (People's Knowledge and Participatory Action Research). *Taking specific phrases, words, ideas, sentences, and flows in the dialogue, I have interpreted them into the wider contexts that I explored with others. I shared these re-contextualizations with the original author(s) and, in some cases, we developed the poems further together. I have worked in this way many times and consider it an insightful and empowering joy for both participating parties.*

Keywords: social justice, diversity, equality, participatory action research, people's knowledge

BlueJam – a portrait of the artist (Credit: Onashile Artists)

http://dx.doi.org/10.3362/9781780449395.006

The struggle

So much conscience consciousness conflict
So much struggle
If I had a genie I'd seek three body doubles
Or two and a sense of humour like Barney Rubble's
Hubble bubble embrace the struggle
What's worth fighting for requires more than war
Still many die for
Be free, conform, be a good sport
Even Oxford's cutting edge thoughts
caught short by the Elite's Tidal force
access fees soar inexorably North

Profit motive pours enough scorn upon the yolk
The townsfolk choke any notion of revolt
Even Rihanna's Umbrella proffers no cold comfort
Arrested dreams and impotent hopes of being paid in Golden Summers
Innate powers become as ash
Pockets stashed full of currencies
We don't even know how to spend

Seek solace in the shallow pool of the inner knowing fool
Be the exception; yet know how far to bend the rule
Before purse strings cut loose
Choose is the soul muscle
Up for a struggle of the ilk of
Madiba's or Tollpuddle
Or will those atomic rumbles be muzzled
By acquiescence with slaveries' customs

Or like Custer muster the gusto for one last go
Undo the residue of feeling confused devalued
Use your unique tools, mine your mind gems
Unearth your fervour and prefer not to wait for change
Be it like Maya set your caged bird free

Soulful humans with a womb full of improvements
Refuel community's rudiments
Not perfect yet brimming with purpose
Insane dreamers change makers
Shape what the creator gave you
Rule breakers

Uplift the masses as we art uplifted
Gifted with a flame, appearance ever changing
Source always same remaining

State of grace where life's a stage
Hounds and hungry horses whisper in corridors

It's no different than 2,000 years before
When the son of man chased the
Moneybrokers out the temple door
At this fissure the universality of Universities
Lacy undies are on the floor
As consumers are defiled via every orifice
By the material Minotaur

Coloured folk are so colourful

We have to be vibrance is helpful
When you can't see the hoops
You have to jump through
The puddles of otherness
To muddle through
'Black folk are so funky'
It's a bodily expression
That lessens; mitigates
The rage
A societally acceptable cloak; a way of saying

Fuck you Fuck me
Without getting labelled uppity
'They're always so so creative'
When your sense of place
Is erased because you don't look the same
When your safety's endangered by both
Strangers and nascent Neo Nazi neighbours
When you're treated like aliens in your workplace
Because in your Tupperware's differing tastes

And the only way to integrate is play Uncle Sam
Like Louis Armstrong smile snap fingers and sing along
Or you don't express natural frustrations
At the rigours of the day in a so-called civilized way
The same Civility that blithely plundered African
Minerals mysticism and rituals
Raped her maidens, flailed and feigned ignorance
As the offspring colonised your bloodline
So blowback was only a matter of time

When you perceive you need to be twice
As keen as the natives to even stand still
Placate just for second class place

In what after all is a rat race
When blatant racists invade your space
Whilst you wait for a night bus with
The one you love and your mates
Just tryin' to get to your gates
You're chased and laid to waste
Machete embedded in your skull
Stormtrooper boots cave in your face
Vital organs strafed by a serrated blade

You're grateful for dexterity of thought
Resilient mind
Fiery heart athletic stature
To deflect mediate obliterate the hate

'Ohhh you lot have such great skin teeth and rhythm'
AKA gonna treat you like a minion
Cool's a crude euphemism for your intelligence
Is deficient for our superior systems
First up you ain't white we ain't black
Stop viewing your fellow woman and man
Through hate's cataracts

Creation's rays manifest a blessed array
Of hues and shades that we might appreciate
And celebrate our similarities through our difference
Besides our ancestors' bloodlines
Knowledge systems
Intuitions and practices
Were plundered and appropriated
To create the basis of much
That racists crave

So Arts and Humanities
Is the title just vanity
Unconsciously concocting colonies
Or at the vanguard
Of natural rebalancing

It's not charity it's parity
The only required reparation
Eradication of disparaging narratives
Of savages cannibals
Cattle assets tax deductible
Colourful chappies and characters

Adequate actors gifted the occasional Academy
Dalliances Dandies

Angst addled bohemian fantasies
Unsalaried rights redactable
Randy Eye Candy

Quit deceiving with facile flattery
Give back the rods cast of African rare earth minerals
And when you leave
Clean the seas
And we'll see which bird rises first
To catch the worm that earns returns
Of the richest Vitamin D&E King Fishes

Famine (PAR)

In school playgrounds...youth clubs and nitty gritty inner city streets
Participatory action research P.A.R.
Means to ignore

And that's how Asha Ali felt for sure
Scorned jaw floored
Yet her displeasure caused researchers' academic status to soar
As the cohort gorged on the results of classical rigour

Future funding points assured as the very intermediaries
AHRC seek to free from the conceits of knowledge elitism
Reel from the familiar feeling of their heads
Embedded in glass ceilings

So consequently we're all like Del and Rodney doing equestrian sports
Only who are the fools and who are the pedigree horses

Here's the water shall we drink or think
Create distance or links
Connect communities or collect data and preserve
The research Omerta

Is the true purpose the transfer of knowledge to contexts where it makes a
difference or to eloquently arraign the untrained with diffidence
Ambivalence
Or assistance in deliverance of interdependent resilience
They're willing and jus require some trust and up-skilling
An innovative communal building
With a big fat till in
Then we can chill and watch it filling
Redistribute the booty to groups of youths crudely subsumed in creativity
Cauterizing cocoons like refugee status
Who just like you in truth enrich our communities

When they feel free
Equal and valued
Some of we be privileged
Privy
As to the true meaning of big society and the imminence of unequivo-
cal disparities designed specifically to enshrine an unbridgeable schism
of pernicious recidivism into every echelon of both state and private
systems

Binding millions of inimitable individuals to exist as disparate minions
administering perpetual plenary poverty for a disenfranchised majority abolishing the promise of meritocracy throttling the benevolent
opulence of an organically evolving democracy of knowledge rights
and resources

For as we breathe local London authorities are in the process of stealth class
cleansing homeless sentient souls

Bereft and powerless as rents are set to jet in a trajectory that reflects the title
of buck wild Harry Styles and his eponymous globe-trotting adolescents

One direction

And that direction's well-being fleeing ascension

Plus the stun to cum from abrupt welfare cuts that will expunge sum from
Londinium as far as Merthyr Tydfil or Hull

I could digress and express more
Yet neither you nor I require another politicized rantifesto

So Arts and Humanities don't lab rat examine we
Like Bob Jam with we
Seek to manage
Augment
Supplement
Harness
Challenge we
Set we free

From a phalanx of acronyms that would have
Bamber Gascoigne scrambling

For as with you
As with me
As with all seven billion plus of we
We're in pursuit of passionate participation
Parity
And
Peace

The Coming Age of We

Fate karma luck synchronicity
Passion will tenacity serendipity
Vital energies for ascendancy
Towards the art of humanity
AKA the age of we

From a plethora of war torn shores
Through Londinium
To the citadel where minds get well fed
Edinburgh's University

Adversity has mercy up its sleeve
So the passion that Asha Ali and Uncle G cultivated
Motivated like photosynthesis
Activated stimulated by
An educated Druid of the light
A light Druid fluent in the science of
Just creative expressive life
Eyes like orange future bright
Like a new dawn like when you
First Wake Lord Tom straddles the battle
Twixt Academic dogma, doctrines and Mantras
With the aplomb of a Shaolin Monk

Fate karma luck synchronicity
Passion will tenacity serendipity
Vital energies for ascendancy
Towards the art of humanity
AKA the age of we

Connections heart wired
Virtual ventricles
Places where the displaced gravitate
A safe space to co-create
To Elevate
Vent
To Alleviate

Was it the hand of fate that harvested the charms of Ijaba
Ismail and Imam marvellous masters at seeing past obstacles
Refuge youth reduce mountains to molehills by sheer will of wills

Was it serendipity that led them to the Mill?
To craft Arts hone skills
Build capacity to take this shit like the Lottery National
Strategize plans to tackle the rigidly rational

To counter attack the red tape rapists
Escape containment fan forward focused flames
From Barnsdale to Harrow narrowing the distance
Tween throbbing Heartists this modern day resistance
Would see off Hitler's fascists
And equip the seemingly disparate
With the facilities to sow seeds of resilience

Fate karma luck synchronicity
Passion will tenacity serendipity
Vital energies for ascendancy
Towards the art of humanity
AKA the age of we

Was it Karma that drew Humanah to Barnsdale's Pastures?
Piper Peter unique being being unique
Heart beats in time with a treasure trove of
Teesside's finest unpolished diamond

Minds hungry to dine on the movement
For spiritual creative economic improvement
Grew thought eagles flew soared spread the word
Observed affirmative brave new worlds
Alternative versions nurtured by diverse earthlings
Determined searching conditions and terms
To pay their way discern their worth
And be reimbursed with just desserts

Fate karma luck synchronicity
Passion will tenacity serendipity
Vital energies for ascendancy
Towards the art of humanity
AKA the age of we

Revolutionary resonations Vybz
Permeated the atmosphere
Garnering soul farmers like Javier
His Latin fire so vital it could even gift me back my hair

Building networks that create hope from despair
Friendships partnerships knowledge from hatred ignorance and fear

And now here we are
We are the age of we are here
Applying our multinational
Unflappable spirit
Tenacious like Hannibal happiness cannibals
Primed to get the disenfranchised out the lurch
With more Enterprise than Spock and Kirk
Real life Thriller filled with action

Like Jackson
Quenching the thirst of
The yes harmed
And yes hurt
Yet still alert
Still got purpose and verve to assert liquid Spiritelligence

Fate karma luck synchronicity
Passion will tenacity serendipity
Vital energies for the ascendancy
Towards the art of humanity
AKA the age of we

Burn our rage into fires of future life incitements
Generation 2013 flirting with the new enlightenment
Think we'll all agree it's a requirement
'Cos some condemn we
Con we
The Con Dem alliance breeds hostile environments

So let's counter the gambit
Of subtle and overt violence
From resource wars guised as
Righteous battles to overthrow evil tyrants

To finance Brokers Banksters Regulators
And what passes for governance
Spin Kings
Rebranding deception into a science
With Saville row's suited impunity

Like Miley twerking with the masses
Halt on the booty
Blind to the beauty

So it's our duty
Amplify what we took time to spy
With our ginormous global eYe
Realize
Fearlessly
Sharing dreams opening hearts
Adapting to the logistics of challenging environs

Like the piercing lucidness of Lucy effusively oozing
Revolutionary energies and utility
Like a Mango and Papaya Smoothie
Or like Diana-Ros our kind of boss
Firm yet tender and fair with a glare
That could take a squadron of Stealth Bombers out the Air

So you
Yes you
Yeah you
Over there
It's your time
To dream
Dare to dream
I dare you

Fate karma luck synchronicity
Passion will tenacity serendipity
Vital energies for ascendancy
Towards the art of humanity
AKA the age of we

Listen to ChriS JaM performing all these poems at: http://www.peoplesknowledge.org/resources

About the author

ChriS JaM participated in several of the authors' and editors' workshops, including the initial meetings as part of the Connected Communities programme. At the time of writing, Chris is collaborating in an outfit which fuses music beats, poetry, and song called *Souldier*, delivering three shows at the 2015 Edinburgh free fringe festival and at local mini-festivals in Manchester. For the last seven years, Chris has project-managed *Wordsmith* (<www.wordsmithawards.com>), which nurtures new generations of writers through poetry projects in schools. He also runs an open mic night 'MiC Bytes' at Jam Street Cafe in Manchester, UK.

CHAPTER 6

A puzzling search for authenticity within academia

*Lucy Pearson, Javier Sanchez Rodriguez and
Asha Ali Mohamed*

Abstract

*What happens when non-academics who, when invited to write an academic paper,
decide to give reasons why they should not write one? This chapter describes why we
felt uncomfortable about writing the paper and what we believe is needed to enable
a process where we can write a paper in a way which reflects our values and vision.
Building on Chapter 2, 'Making connections in the "white-walled labyrinth"', this
chapter provides a critical look at the practice of co-produced research for social justice,
collective writing, and different kinds of knowledge, emphasizing the importance of
creating spaces for genuine dialogue to ensure legitimacy and authenticity, and to
enable processes of agency and emergence.*

Keywords: co-produced research, authenticity, emergence, interdependence,
agency

Background

In July 2014 we, as members of both RefugeeYouth[1] and the Arts and Humanities Research Council-funded Web of Connections project (see 'Making connections in the "white-walled labyrinth"', Guzman et al., 2016), were invited
to write a 500-word abstract to propose a paper we would write about our
experience of what co-produced research can achieve for social justice. The
paper was to be published in this book. In rather a rush, Lucy and Asha wrote
the abstract (see Box 6.1), and everyone from Web of Connections who read
and responded to it seemed to be happy.

We knocked around some ideas about creating a reading group, and we
shared some reading via email, but then we ran out of time and got confused
about what we were doing and why. As a result, we spent a weekend with
the principal investigator, Tom Wakeford, together trying to get our heads
around it.

We picked a paper written by Peter Reason (2006), which explores how
we can judge 'quality' in 'action research' (see Glossary). We read this paper
together and used it to help us talk about our experiences of the work we had

http://dx.doi.org/10.3362/9781780449395.007

Box 6.1 RefugeeYouth's proposal for the paper

RefugeeYouth is working in partnership with four local youth-led community projects – Humanah in Middlesbrough, Teamwork in Birmingham, Mustaqbal in Harrow, and Leeds Dynamic in Leeds. We are working with Edinburgh University and several other academic partners on a participatory action research (PAR) project – the Web of Connection. The project is exploring how a PAR approach can be used to build community. Young people are working together to research the issues that affect them, engaging in creative and collective activity to generate knowledge and learning in order to make positive social change locally and nationally.

We are interested in exploring the value of different types of knowledge, and in particular in finding ways to bridge the gap and redress the inequality between traditional 'elite academic' knowledge and what we call 'roots academic' knowledge.

Our contribution will reflect on what we are learning and how we are using that learning to make change. We will explore the impact on individuals – the participating young researchers and the academics – as well as the impact on the community groups involved and on their work towards social justice in their local communities and nationally. We will offer a multi-perspective reflection on a multi-dimensional project.

We have always been very aware that when we engage with theory many people can become quickly marginalized. A performance for the Arts and Humanities Research Council showcase in Edinburgh that we devised demonstrated how if the process is open and creative everyone can engage – not just those with the confidence to articulate themselves in an academic way.

Our contribution will be created in a way that allows everyone in this project to have a voice in it. Instead of struggling to engage people with a traditional academic process, we will aim to create a process which values, respects and recognizes the power and intelligence of everyone's contribution – whether they wish to express it through poetry, through music, through dance, through film, through speaking or through writing.

Our contribution will value different types of knowledge and language, and show the power of knowledge that comes from different experiences and different cultures. Our aim will be to get this knowledge recognized in the academic sphere, as something of value in the mainstream – not as tokenistic 'youth' or 'cultural' knowledge.

---

been doing, to find new ways to think about the problems and challenges we had faced, and the areas of the work that made us confused, angry and hurt, as well as the areas that made us feel hopeful, inspired, and motivated.

Through this process we realized that we felt discomfort about writing a paper about our project and we started to understand why – that's how we came up with our working title: 'This paper proposes a process for writing a paper that investigates why the proposed paper was not written'.

Addressing the key issues

This title can be broken down into two key questions that we wanted to address:

1. Why did we feel uncomfortable about writing the paper?
2. What are the ingredients we need to enable a process where we can write the paper in a way which reflects our methodology/values/beliefs/vision so that we don't recreate the world that we are trying to change?

We also realized that these are not two separate questions, because in fact the reasons why we didn't write it are also the ingredients that we feel we need to inform our processes. In our abstract (Box 6.1), we said that our contribution would be created by everyone in our project working collectively. This chapter is an exploration of why we have not got to that point yet, and is a reflection on and response to the issues that are alive within the project.

Question 1: Why did we feel uncomfortable about writing the paper?

We felt nervous about just going ahead and writing the paper on other people's behalf, or writing *about* other people. Who were we to try and represent the learning of the whole network? We were trying to understand the legitimacy of what we were doing. But the approach we were taking made us feel like we were in danger of doing the thing that we were against.

Looking back at the first six months of Web of Connections, we realized that we hadn't always managed to create a process that people could understand and with which they could engage. Maybe people weren't engaging because the process wasn't legitimate? People were sending clear messages by opting out of a writing process that was meant to involve everyone. We didn't act on those messages, because the project became driven by deadlines and action plans, not leaving time for exploratory dialogue.

When we co-designed Web of Connections, there were many different agendas and many different partners. Everyone was coming into it with widely varying perspectives, different levels of relationship intensity, and a range of needs that they expected the project to be able to meet.

The original plan for Web of Connections underestimated the time that it takes to build the relationships necessary for a communicative space for genuine dialogue. We had limited time and big ambitions. We thought we could make the project work through structures and teams and roles, but we found the formation of teams and roles harder than we expected. As Reason says (2006: 7), 'The process of drawing people together and creating a framework for collaborative work always takes longer than one imagines. At times building collaboration will seem to get in the way of directly addressing practical problems.'

For many people involved in the project, the idea of undertaking participatory action research (PAR, see Glossary) as the core of the project became a separate task from the work they were doing and from people's ambitions for the project. This is the opposite of what we understand to be the principles behind PAR. In our view, the project will not be fully legitimate until we build authentic engagement with the critical and conscious dimension of the project across the network.

We feel reluctant to write because we think it likely that the way each of us sees the issue will be different. As soon as you commit something to paper it feels like you are saying 'this is the truth', 'this is how it is', whereas we know that there are many truths, and that the work, and the way that we see it, is constantly changing. Therefore it's useful to think of inquiry as something that uses our different perspectives on reality, rather than something that seeks to represent a single reality (Rorty, 1999: 33). 'Living knowledge' is more useful to us, and perhaps for contributing towards greater social justice, than something that claims one truth. This is reflected in the fact that we have found that dialogue processes are much more productive when we genuinely listen to what each other is saying and try to learn from it, rather than each of us simply trying to argue the truth of our own point of view.

Question 2: What are the ingredients we need to enable a process where we can write the paper

Through reflecting on the ups and downs of our work we have learned something about the ingredients we need to create authentic processes for working together. We summarize seven of these here.

Creating a communicative space for dialogue

> This formation of communicative space is in itself a form of action. It may well be that the most important thing we can do in certain situations is to open, develop, maintain, encourage new and better forms of communication and dialogue. (Reason, 2006: 6)

Sometimes we feel the need to use particular processes to help us create a dialogic space, for example, the 'people's circle', which gives everyone equal space to respond to a question or issue, without interruption, one at a time. This can be very useful, because it helps to break the normal dynamics of a group where some people talk too much and some people never talk.

Through the project we have been able to take these 'tools' that we have experienced together back to our own local groups, and they have helped us to create an inclusive environment where we feel we can express ourselves genuinely. We have become more proactive and aware.

However, sometimes we get stuck with the tools, paying too much attention to designing processes rather than making inquiry a way of living. Sometimes if we are in a structured session or workshop we end up saying what we think people want to hear, and we don't feel comfortable saying what we really think and feel. We've found that it has been important for us to pay attention to the informal dialogue that takes place outside our structured activities (such as when some of us go outside for a cigarette), in which people often say what they really think. This is recognized in the fact that often even the non-smokers go outside with the smokers! Sometimes people are seeking reassurance, which gives them the confidence to go back inside and say what they really think.

It's also important to try and make sure that these informal dialogues don't undermine the more structured spaces we have for collective decision-making. There is a danger that those people who don't go outside for a cigarette become excluded from key elements of the dialogue. It's then that our processes become illegitimate. Our challenge is always to try to bring the cigarette conversations into the people's circle. We've found it important to remind ourselves that the purpose of techniques such as the people's circle should be to make them no longer necessary. We should try to learn how to make authentic engagement and embed it in the way we live and work.

Finding legitimacy through authentic engagement

Web of Connections is made up of a wide variety of people. Almost everyone has experienced suffering at some point in their lives. Yet, in dialogue processes there is a danger that we only react to the suffering that we can relate to our own lives. That is because we can often see ourselves as different and unconnected. When we find ways of creating common ground – perhaps a theme in common between us – it enables us to engage with each other as humans and to understand each other's suffering. A great example of this was the Women's Circle residential, which brought together a diverse group of young women from London and Middlesbrough for a weekend; it was a powerful experience which had a great impact on those involved. Through a mix of informal and structured processes, women from very different backgrounds and experiences came together and built relationships and learned about and understood each other's struggles (see 'Examining our differences', Mohamed et al., 2016).

Each of us does a lot of planning for our workshops and residentials, but we have learned that sometimes *not* sticking to the plan is really important; in order for engagement to be genuine, we have to change the plan in response to what emerges through our work.

We felt we didn't want to write a paper about our work yet, because we didn't feel that we had by then created enough communicative spaces where we could have authentic engagement. People need to *want* to engage with critical reflection on their work. We need to feel that this is relevant and useful to our lives.

We looked back at *Becoming a Londoner* (RefugeeYouth, 2009) and reflected on the process that developed that publication. We felt there was authentic engagement at the heart of it. This is reflected in the back cover, which lists all the different people who were involved in different ways at different stages of the process. What was written emerged through an ongoing process, which did not end when the book was finished. The writing served as a way of capturing the learning from different aspects of the work, helping us to understand it better ourselves and enabling us to share it with others.

Being aware about our choices and their consequences

We need to be aware of the choices we are making and consider their consequences (Reason, 2006: 3). Authentic engagement means engaging people in making choices and thinking about the consequences. Consensus isn't just about everyone saying *yes*; people need to understand, and express, why they are saying yes or, potentially, *no*: 'The legitimacy of any conclusions and decisions reached by participants will be proportional to the degree of authentic engagement of those concerned' (Kemmis, 2001: 100).

Sometimes it felt like we lost that legitimacy. For example, on the final day of the second national gathering of the Web of Connections project, we rushed the process of getting everyone to sign up to teams and roles within the project, and everyone said *yes* to things without being aware of what they were signing up to. As a result the decision-making was not fully 'conscious', in the sense used by Paulo Freire.[2] The lack of time also meant that people weren't fully aware of the consequences of the choices they were making.

At other times, we felt that we were becoming more aware of our choices and their consequences. This is demonstrated in a comment from Humanah Youth, the project partner in Middlesbrough:

> Another great thing is that we have started to bring conscious learning into action; for example we are more conscious around ourselves. I have seen this in a few people in Humanah. Like we are stepping back and looking at our lives and seeing why are we doing something and how can we do things differently.

Making sure both agency and communion are present

Marshall (1984:65) writes, 'Agency is the expression of independence through self-protection, self-assertion and self-expansion; communion seeks union and cooperation as its way of coming to terms with uncertainty'.

The mainstream culture in which we are operating is driven by *agency* (see Glossary) – an individualistic, capitalist approach, where success is measured by individual achievement and wealth. We, on the other hand, are trying to make *communality* central to our working processes, as we see all around us the inequality and oppression that an agentic approach creates.

However, we also recognize that agency is important – being the individual's ability to act and make changes to their own situation. In fact, agency and communion are potential complements rather than alternatives (Marshall, 1984). Can we expect people to act on the problems of the world until their own survival needs are met? Until people feel they have 'agency' at an individual level, how can they take the step to work in 'communion' with others?

Maslow's 'hierarchy of needs' (Maslow, 1943; Wikipedia, 2016) maps out the order in which our needs must be met in order for us to have agency, or 'self-actualization'. There is some interesting criticism of this model that actually opposes the idea of a hierarchical order for these needs (Max-Neef, et al. 1989; Wahba and Bridwell, 1976). In short, why is any one of our needs more fundamental than another?

We need to be invested in the struggle for social justice on a personal level, rather than making it about 'helping others'. For example, if we view the people we work with as 'clients' rather than fellow human beings, we detach ourselves from our world. Josephine Klein (1995: 7) talks about this need for attachment as empathic imagination.

Martin Luther King (1963) reminds us of the importance of not separating the individual from the wider world: 'We must be concerned not merely about who murdered them, but about the system, the way of life, the philosophy which produced the murderers.'

To co-produce knowledge that contributes to social justice, we need to ask ourselves an important question: do our individual and collective beliefs provide a reliable guide to getting what we want? (Rorty, 1999). Before we can answer that we need to find out what our shared beliefs are. We must also share a picture of where we want to be. To build a shared vision we need to engage in collective dreaming – the 'communion' mentioned by Marshall. In order to do this we must all bring ourselves – our individual 'agency' – to the table. We can't and should not expect to be the same, feel the same, act the same – indeed we are powerful when we act together precisely because we are *not* the same. In this process, agency and communion are not merely complementary, but actually *interdependent*.

Understanding the interdependence of 'me', 'us', and 'the world'

In his discussion of different approaches to action research, Reason talks about researchers operating at first-, second-, and third-person levels (2006: 1). He talks about these as separate concepts. However, reflecting on our work, we see these levels as reflecting 'me', 'us', and the 'wider world' as part of the same concept of PAR. To achieve authentic engagement, we need to be consciously operating at all three levels.

We need to understand our own reality in order to connect to our communities, and then to connect ourselves to the wider world. We need to understand our own privileges before we can engage with other people's suffering. A humane world can only happen when we can all connect to suffering that does not have the same face as ours.

> If I try to help before I understand who I am in the situation, then I am not likely to help. There is a danger of "helping" in a way that isn't helpful because it is controlling or patronising or suffocating, or just doesn't understand. (Reason, 2006: 7)

If you don't bring your own reality to the table, and I don't bring mine, and if we don't acknowledge and explore them, how can we expect to work together – let alone help anyone else?

Equally, if we try to make change for ourselves, without understanding the wider world context we are operating within, and the power structures and dynamics that impact on us, then we are unlikely to achieve much.

We need to constantly reflect on our own reality; the reality of the people we are working with; and the realities of the wider world. We can only define ourselves in relation to others. The discourses around us are what help us to figure out what we believe.

One of the strengths of RefugeeYouth has been that we are constantly moving between these three levels. The July 2013 Arts and Humanities Research Council showcase event in Edinburgh demonstrated the power of this approach. Through drama, dance, poetry, and music, young people from London, Middlesbrough, Birmingham, and Scotland came together to share their experiences and formulated a collective piece which was a powerful representation of individual and collective experience. By learning about other people's experiences we were better able to reflect on our own experiences, and through pooling our knowledge we were better able to understand the context we were living in.

We realized that if there is a gap between what is written and the people and communities who are being written about, then what is written loses its legitimacy (if we are coming, as *we* are, from the perspective of wanting to use research to achieve social justice). Separating 'me', 'us', and the 'wider world' can end up reinforcing the divisions and power dynamics that already exist.

Turning feelings into learning

We know that learning doesn't just happen in the classroom (in fact, sometimes it doesn't happen there at all), and that some of the most important and powerful learning comes from lived experience. One of the most powerful aspects of working together through this project is that we all bring so much different knowledge, because we have all had such different life experiences.

However, experiences generate feelings and feelings can either enable or block learning:

> We collect … information through our senses, and then hold the knowing inside ourselves as feelings. In some instances we are able to translate these feelings into conceptual knowledge that gives insight into the ways which our oppression is maintained. But often this translation work is not done, and nevertheless we walk around potent with this knowledge. (Douglas, 2002: 250)

We have found that sometimes the feelings burn inside us and make us angry. Negative feelings can be really destructive in this way and it is at this point that listening is so important. If we don't listen to each other – really listen – then we get angry and frustrated and these feelings block our learning, and stop us from taking action. But we can be even less likely to evaluate the positive feelings. We enjoy when something works well, but we forget to analyse how and why it worked – what were the ingredients?

In fact, on typing up our discussions, we realized we reflected far more on the negative experiences and feelings than the positive ones. We concluded that we also need to write about what has worked – the moments where we have felt that we *are* doing what we say, and where there *is* authentic engagement.

Recognizing emergence

We sense that there is often a gap between the way we say things are and the way they actually are. This can lead us to feel that we are just 'talking the talk', 'bullshitting' or 'talking rubbish'. We must acknowledge this gap and engage in constant critical reflection on what we wish things to be and what they are. We need a balance: being self-critical, but not so critical that it's self-destructive.

> The process of inquiry is as important as specific outcomes. Good action research emerges over time in an evolutionary and developmental process, as individuals develop skills of inquiry and as communities of inquiry develop within communities of practice. (Reason and Bradbury, 2001: p.11)

Conclusion

In conclusion, the opportunity to write for this book has helped us to think about how we write, who writes, and why. The theory we have read has helped us reflect and understand, and what we have written has already started a deeper and more honest dialogue amongst the Web of Connection. We would like to build on this learning and develop a collective process which incorporates the ingredients listed in this chapter, so as to capture and share the learning from our project in an authentic way.

Notes

1. RefugeeYouth is a small national charity dedicated to overcoming isolation, alienation, and despair among young refugees by supporting opportunities for their development, inclusion, and integration. See RefugeeYouth (2016) for more information.
2. Critical consciousness (*conscientização* in Portuguese). See Freire, 1970.

References

Douglas, C. (2002) 'Using co-operative inquiry with black women managers: exploring possibilities for moving from surviving to thriving', *Systemic Practice and Action Research* 15: 249–62 <http://dx.doi.org/10.1023/A:1016396526167>.

Freire, P. (1970) *Pedagogy of the Oppressed*, Penguin Books, London.

Guzman, M., Kadima, C., Lovell, G., Mohamed, A.A., Norton, R., Rivas, F. and Thiam, A. (2016) 'Making connections in the "white-walled labyrinth"', in People's Knowledge Editorial Collective (eds), *People's Knowledge and Participatory*

Action Research: Escaping the White-Walled Labyrinth, pp. 23–32, Practical Action Publishing, Rugby <http://dx.doi.org/10.3362/9781780449395.003>.

Kemmis, S. (2001) 'Exploring the relevance of critical theory for action research: emancipatory action research in the footsteps of Jürgen Habermas', in P. Reason and H. Bradbury (eds), *Handbook of Action Research: Participative Inquiry and Practice*, pp. 91–102, Sage Publications, London.

King Jr, M.L. (1963) 'Eulogy for the martyred children', Speech delivered on 18 September 1963 at Sixth Avenue Baptist Church, Birmingham, AL, <http://www.drmartinlutherkingjr.com/birminghamchurchbombingeulogy.htm> [accessed 26 August 2016].

Klein, J. (1995) *Doubts and Certainties in the Practice of Psychotherapy*, Karnac, London.

Marshall, J. (1984) *Women Managers: Travellers in a Male World*, Wiley, Chichester.

Maslow, A.H. (1943) 'A theory of human motivation', *Psychological Review* 50: 370–96.

Max-Neef, M.A., Elizalde, A. and Hopenhayn, M. (1989) 'Development and human needs', in M.A. Max-Neef, with A. Elizalde and M. Hopenhayn (eds), *Human Scale Development: Conception, Application and Further Reflections*, pp. 13-54, The Apex Press, New York, NY.

Mohamed, A.A., Istwani, A., Villate, B., Ohberg, E., Galante, E., Mohamed, F., Ahmed, I., Smith, H.M., Pearson, L., Guzman, M., Istwani, S., Sakar, S., Hunter-Darch, S. and Miah, T. (2016) 'Examining our differences', in People's Knowledge Editorial Collective (eds), *People's Knowledge and Participatory Action Research: Escaping the White-Walled Labyrinth*, pp. 33–44, Practical Action Publishing, Rugby <http://dx.doi.org/10.3362/9781780449395.004>.

Reason, P. (2006) 'Choice and quality in action research practice', *Journal of Management Inquiry* 15: 187–203.

Reason, P. and Bradbury, H. (2001) 'Inquiry and participation in search of a world worthy of human aspiration', in P. Reason and H. Bradbury (eds), *Handbook of Action Research: Participative Inquiry and Practice*, pp. 1–14, Sage Publications, London.

RefugeeYouth (2009) *Becoming A Londoner*, RefugeeYouth, London <http://www.refugeeyouth.org/wp-content/uploads/2016/06/Becoming-ALondoner_LoRes.pdf> [accessed 26 August 2016].

Rorty, R. (1999) *Philosophy and Social Hope*, Penguin Books, London.

Wahba, M.A. and Bridwell, L.G. (1976) 'Maslow reconsidered: a review of research on the need hierarchy theory,' *Organizational Behavior and Human Performance* 15: 212–40, <http://dx.doi.org/10.1016/0030-5073(76)90038-6>.

Wikipedia (2016) 'Maslow's hierarchy of needs', <https:// en.wikipedia.org/wiki/Maslow%27s_hierarchy_of_needs> [accessed 6 August 2016].

About the authors

Lucy Pearson, Javier Sanchez Rodriguez, and **Asha Ali Mohamed** are or were members of RefugeeYouth.

CHAPTER 7

Community media and cultural politics on Tyneside

Hugh Kelly with Graham Jeffery

Abstract

How can we ensure, in the process of using participatory film-making for social transformation, that community voices are authentic and representative? I have collaborated with an academic to write a commentary on a film which draws on 30 years of using video inclusively in North East England. The film depicts the persistent problems of poverty, exclusion, and long-term unemployment. The authors unpack and interrogate claims that narratives of individual and social transformation are being inflated, and explore the role of participatory film-making and community media as research methods. They highlight the value of collaborative relationships between film-makers and communities as they explore the powers that shape people's lives. Integral to this chapter is a 30-minute film: Remaking Society: Communities on the Edge (Swingbridge Media 2013).*

Keywords: participatory film-making, community media, representation, authenticity, conscientization

Introduction

As a film-maker and fine arts graduate, my first community arts project was to make a documentary with photographs and video with young people who were experiencing unemployment in Scotswood, a town in the county of Tyneside in North East England in the late 1970s. My aim was to provide the means for people to represent their own situations, stories, and neighbourhoods, particularly by providing access to media tools.

My practice was rooted in a radical politics of participation. At its core was a critique of hegemonic narratives of 'exclusion' and the tendency of the local (and national) state to reproduce inequalities, even within policies and programmes ostensibly designed to alleviate the effects of poverty (see, for example, Community Development Project, 1977).

For the following 35 years, I chronicled some major changes in North East England with Swingbridge Media, the film and multimedia collective I founded – making documents of significance in the social histories of Gateshead and Tyneside. As a collective, we involved many residents of estates

http://dx.doi.org/10.3362/9781780449395.008

The authors in conversation at the Tyneside Cinema, June 2013

Video drama workshop. Scotswood, Newcastle upon Tyne, 1980

and neighbourhoods in the area in producing media texts that represented their lives – from *An English Estate* (1992) to *Poverty – It's a Crime* (2001), *Tackling Poverty* (2012), and other recent work which explores participation in cultural activities and the involvement of young people in the spectacular new developments on the Gateshead Quays (Swingbridge Media, 1992, 2001, 2012, 2016).

Les Sreedhar and Andy Dumble in a scene from *An English Estate*, 1992. Photograph by Steve Conlan

Yet, alongside official narratives of creative civic participation and international cultural tourism, there remain persistent problems of exclusion, poverty, and long-term unemployment – a 'combination of deprivation and spectacle', as my academic collaborator Graham Jeffery (2005: 25) has put it, which is double-edged and complex.

The transition to a post-industrial economy in the North East, with a huge shift within a quarter-century from a heavy manufacturing/mining base to a services and 'knowledge economy', has forced adaptation and change on working-class communities ill-equipped to cope with the consequences of such a rapid shift. Formal education/training systems and community infrastructure have been slow to keep up, and the lived experience of this painful transition has tended to be downplayed in official narratives of 'regeneration' and 'neighbourhood renewal'.

With part-funding from the Arts and Humanities Research Council Connected Communities 'pilot demonstrator' fund, the Remaking Society project enabled Graham and I to explore the archive of Swingbridge Media's work. This acted as a stimulus to debate the role of participatory photography, film, and video as a tool for the co-production of research with members of communities often represented as excluded, marginal, or disadvantaged. We organized public screenings at the Tyneside Cinema, each followed by debate and discussion, of selected excerpts from my archive under two titles: *Tackling Poverty* and *Whose Culture is it Anyway?*

We made a short film, *Remaking Society* (Swingbridge Media, 2013), designed to act as a provocation. In it we discuss the evolution of Swingbridge Media's collaborations and revisit some of the filming locations, including the site of the Saltmeadows and Old Fold communities just south-east of Gateshead Quays, which has now been almost entirely demolished. We intercut footage from films made in the early and late 1990s with images from 2013 to demonstrate the scale of the 'remaking'/redevelopment that has been undertaken: a story that is often forgotten in the rush to celebrate the 'regeneration' of Gateshead through an iconic culture-led waterfront development.

Community media as a research method? Issues and problems

An important methodological precursor for 'co-production' of cultural artefacts, texts, and research with communities comes from the work of the community arts and media movement. However, the claims made for community media strategies, which are frequently characterized by inflated narratives of transformation, of powerful personal or social change, or of large-scale 'social impact', need to be unpacked and interrogated. There is a growing academic interest in 'socially engaged' arts and media, alongside an emerging literature on activism, art, and urban change (see Kester, 2004; Bishop, 2012; Parry et al., 2012; Buser and Arthurs, 2013). Some of the most interesting work takes place at the intersection of different practices, such as participatory arts/media and community-based action research.

The ideological force field in which participatory work takes place – in practice and research – is complex and contested, and one of the values of interrogating the archive has been in opening up a debate about the inherent tensions in working 'with communities', and digging into the problems of representation, authenticity, and power relations in this collaboration.

The first methodological argument concerns the development of collaborative relationships between the documentary film-maker and communities. At the core of this is the notion of 'empowerment' – fashionable in the 1970s and early 1980s, but used less in the lexicon of community media in the present day. This is empowerment in the sense of providing access to media training, of skills sharing, and of providing the means, via media, to represent and transmit stories and points of view. Informed by a radical politics of community as negotiation of co-existence, as a condition of interdependence, and as *emergent* (see Glossary), this might even, in the 1970s, have been called 'consciousness-raising' or, in Freire's terms, 'conscientization' (see Lloyd, 1972).

This approach has informed my work on poverty and exclusion very strongly. Many of the films that deal with issues faced by communities living with poverty have sought to enable the telling of 'the other side of the story', and this has partly been achieved by placing participants into positions of power within the film-making process and negotiating with participants about the ways in which stories are told. For example, a young man who was subsequently demonized in the popular press as 'Spider Boy', who had undertaken a string of burglaries and assaults and was eventually convicted of manslaughter, had direct involvement in the process of making *Poverty – It's a Crime*. He participates as an interviewer – as the person behind the microphone asking the questions – rather than being represented as a criminal thug. These kinds of role inversions are common within community media practice – and provide counter-narratives as well as practical strategies for 'inclusion'.

Linked to this approach are critical pedagogies of participation, as theorized, for example, by Freire (Lloyd,1972) and Giroux (1992). These have been developed in practical ways by community media activists who have explored the use of community media as a form of informal adult education – as portals to further training, of skills development, and developing what might be called 'trajectories of participation' – building forms of community out of arts and media practices.

A key shift since the 1970s has been the influence of technology, which is gradually transforming society by creating a vehicle for different voices to be heard. There have been successive waves of change in available technological tools, altering modes of access to media – through community radio and television, citizen journalism, and the shifts in participation enabled through the internet and social media.

The emergence of community media access centres in the 1970s/80s – a tradition within which the work of Swingbridge Media itself was situated – was tied up with other forms of social activism, attempting to address issues of housing, poverty, racism, and unemployment. This is community action 'about what had not been sorted out'; it took a stance against 'top down' solutions – in which media tools were allied to a campaigning/ activism function – exposing power relationships, e.g. in directly confronting issues of policing or in drawing attention to the social consequences of unemployment.

In the 1990s, with the advent of single regeneration budgets and New Labour in 1997, some of these explicitly oppositional media tactics were softened – one can perhaps even say *incorporated* – as government commissioning bodies began to make use of community media techniques as commissioned tools for consultation and neighbourhood planning.

The series of films made by Swingbridge Media in the late 1990s, in which young people were involved in 'documenting the changes' to their neighbourhoods, walk more of an ideological tightrope than the earlier, more campaigning works, which were not commissioned by local government or regeneration agencies. This incorporation of social/community media strategies as a communications, 'audience development', or even marketing tool by government agencies and cultural institutions raises some interesting questions about the extent to which radical, critical forms of participatory practice can survive, especially as they too become professionalized, more dependent upon state funding, or scaled up/more ambitious – and inevitably less 'independent'. However, the same tensions often apply to universities or funding councils that seek to demonstrate 'community engagement' and 'impact'. In both settings, one way round this dilemma can be to explicitly address the ethics of such public engagement in practice (see Guzman et al., 2016; Pearson et al., 2016; Wakeford, 2016).

Swingbridge Media's later work, in particular some of the commissioned promotional films for Sage Gateshead and for cultural education programmes in the North East (*NE Generation*, 2009–12), mirror some of these contradictions and problems well, despite their continued use of participatory methods in their development and production. One way of examining the profound shifts in the North East economy could be to see the whole process as a huge rebranding and communications exercise – as memorably critiqued in Jonathan Meades' (2005) broadside against the regeneration industry in *Abroad Again: On the Brandwagon*. To what extent have community media practitioners been complicit in this sort of rebranding? Where is the space for 'independent' or radical media in this landscape/brandscape, of 'capitals of culture' and culture-led regeneration? What is the role of academic/community research in reframing and analysing some of these shifts and ambiguities?

The backlash against participatory and community arts

In the 1970s and 1980s, audio and video equipment was expensive; now it's relatively cheap, and many community members – but not all – have access to tools, platforms, and the potential (if not always the time or inclination) to produce their own content. This raises the question of the space occupied by *critical* social media. Widespread access to social media means almost everyone can 'produce content', but where are the critical voices? There is also an increasing blurriness between 'official' and 'alternative' media as social media tools, swarming online conversations, interactivity, and social journalism become the norm. Within these 'big conversations', however, there are many voices that are hardly heard, especially those of the less advantaged.

Peter Stark, one of the cultural architects of the Gateshead Quays development, was asked, 'What is the Baltic [the new Gateshead art gallery] for? What relationship will it have with people in the Old Fold, Saltmeadows, etc.?' He replied absolutely decisively that, 'This is not going to be a community arts project'. It's interesting in this context to see the word 'community' used almost as a term of abuse – as representing poor quality, inferior, local, or parochial forms of culture. Underlying this attitude is perhaps a 'deficit' model of 'community art', standing in contrast to prestigious 'international contemporary art'. The democratic language of 'community art', rooted in the everyday, stands in contrast to the sometimes arcane terminology employed by those who frame contemporary art in the media – and the academics who are employed to talk about it. Grayson Perry (2013) explored what he calls 'international art English' in his 2013 BBC Reith Lectures:

> Now this international art English began in the 1960s in art magazines and then it very quickly spread like wildfire because everybody wanted to be thought of as being very serious about the art, and so it spread to institutions, commercial galleries, even students' dissertations, you'll see

it in today. Now the non-fluent in this kind of language might feel a bit uneducated and they might ... think you might need to understand this in order to pass judgment. I just want to tell you now, you don't. I mean particularly when we are confronted with conceptual art that might be like a little bit of text on a scrappy bit of paper on the wall or a black and white fuzzy photo, well in the 1970s that was what conceptual art looked like ... Now I think a lot of these artworks are luxury goods ... You know there's a new breed of collector now where buying art is just an extension of you know you get the Ferrari, and then you'll go and get a nice handbag and then you'll go and pick up a big shiny bit of art to put on, in the front of the house. You know that's the way it is ... And the whole idea of quality seems to be a sort of contested word now like you're buying into this sort of, the language of the elite by saying oh that's very good or something, you know ... But then again I might say well what do I judge them against? Do I judge them against government policy?

Community meets the Millennium Bridge

Various aspects of Swingbridge Media's films address the changes on Tyneside. One sequence stands out: footage shot in 1998/9 of the massive steel frame of the

The Gateshead Millennium Bridge being built - from *Extending East Gateshead*

Millennium Bridge moving gracefully down the Tyne before being craned into place, cut together with a soundtrack of a young woman from East Gateshead singing about 'Hollywood dreams' in a karaoke session in a working men's club; the club and the streets that surround it have since been demolished, but Newcastle-Gateshead's own 'South Bank' is now firmly established. This single sequence in the film conjures together many of the complicated issues about the industrial heritage of North East England making way for a different kind of economy. It raises questions about what all these rhetorics of 'creativity' and cultural participation are *for*. Perhaps it also asks whether the value of skilled, craft, manual labour is evaporating as the so-called new/knowledge/creative economy is superimposed on working-class communities. Symbolic totems of an industrial past (the Baltic Flour Mills, the entirely symbolic remnants of cranes, docks, and quaysides) are being repurposed for contemporary art and culture.

Yet, the later films also explore the mission of the cultural institutions to promote engagement and participation. They expose some of the ambiguities in deploying a culture-led strategy for regeneration, especially when the material conditions of many of Tyneside's poorest communities have, arguably, not altered substantially in 30 years.

A further methodological issue concerns who the 'audience' is for these sorts of community films and videos, and what happens in the process of screening and rescreening the films? How does the context in which they are presented affect their reception? For whom are they made? A key element of the technique involves screening the films back to those who are involved in their making – and the use of media to provoke, question, and stimulate debate.

Young woman singing karaoke in a working men's club - screen grab from *Extending East Gateshead*

A scene from *Tackling Poverty*, 2012 - Jane Scandle with son and mother. Photograph by Hugh Kelly

The future promise of community media

The ideologies of community media remain contingent on the contexts in which they take place. They can produce partial and eminently questionable results. However, we would suggest that some of the techniques and approaches developed through this work retain value on five levels:

1. as a means of opening up dialogues between different sections of the community
2. as a means of asking questions about the relative value placed on different kinds of cultural production across the communities of the North East
3. as a means of developing critical dialogue between academics, activists, artists, and residents
4. as a way of creating new public discourses which challenge some of the common orthodoxies of 'regeneration' and 'poverty', including the tendency of mass media (and right-wing politicians) to spectacularize or demonize those people living in conditions of deprivation
5. as a way of bringing to the surface experiential knowledge and accounts of communities living on the edge, and validating/representing lived experience in more subtle and nuanced ways.

References

Bishop, C. (2012) *Artificial Hells: Participatory Art and the Politics of Spectatorship*, Verso, London.

Buser, M. and Arthurs, J. (2013) *Cultural Activism in the Community*, Arts and Humanities Research Council, Swindon.

Community Development Project (1977) *Gilding the Ghetto: The State and the Poverty Experiments*, HMSO, London. Available from: <http://indiamond6.ulib.iupui.edu/cdm/ref/collection/CDP/id/3506> [accessed 8 August 2016].

Giroux, H. (1992) *Border Crossings: Cultural Workers and the Politics of Education*, Routledge, London.

Guzman, M., Kadima, C., Lovell, G., Mohamed, A.A., Norton, R., Rivas, F. and Thiam, A. (2016) 'Making connections in the "white-walled labyrinth"', in People's Knowledge Editorial Collective (eds), *People's Knowledge and Participatory Action Research: Escaping the White-Walled Labyrinth*, pp. 23–32, Practical Action Publishing, Rugby <http://dx.doi.org/10.3362/9781780449395.003>.

Jeffery, G. (ed.) (2005) *The Creative College: Building a Successful Learning Culture in the Arts*, Trentham Books, Stoke on Trent.

Kester, G. (2004) *Conversation Pieces: Community and Communication in Modern Art*, University of California Press, Berkeley, CA.

Lloyd, A. (1972) 'Freire, conscientization and adult education', *Adult Education Quarterly* 23: 3–20.

Meades, J. (2005) *Abroad Again: On the Brandwagon* [film], BBC2 TV. Available at: <www.youtube.com/watch?v=A8MEm3eVPNU> [accessed 25 August 2016].

Parry, B. (ed.) with Medlyn, S. and Tahir, M. (2012) *Cultural Hijack: Rethinking Intervention*, Liverpool University Press, Liverpool.

Pearson, L., Sanchez Rodriguez, J. and Mohamed, A.A. (2016) 'A puzzling search for authenticity within academia', in People's Knowledge Editorial Collective (eds), *People's Knowledge and Participatory Action Research: Escaping the White-Walled Labyrinth*, pp. 63–72, Practical Action Publishing, Rugby <http://dx.doi.org/10.3362/9781780449395.007>.

Perry, G. (2013) 'Democracy has bad taste' [radio], BBC Reith Lectures, 'Grayson Perry: Playing to the Gallery' Lecture 1, <www.bbc.co.uk/programmes/b03969vt> [accessed 8 August 2016].

Swingbridge Media (1992) *An English Estate* [film], broadcast on Channel 4 TV <https://www.youtube.com/watch?v=Lr-iZi6FEWo> [accessed 26 August 2016].

Swingbridge Media (2001) *Poverty – It's a Crime* [film], <https://www.youtube.com/watch?v=735uIzTK4f0> [accessed 26 August 2016].

Swingbridge Media (2012) *Tackling Poverty* [film], <https://www.youtube.com/watch?v=vmlqwInt8NE> [accessed 26 August 2016].

Swingbridge Media (2013) *Remaking Society: Communities on the Edge* [film], <https://youtu.be/zrBgT51cz18> [accessed 9 August 2016].

Swingbridge Media (2016) 'Welcome to Swingbridge Media' <http://www.swingbridgemedia.co.uk/> [accessed 26 August 2016].

Wakeford, T. (2016) 'Signposts for people's knowledge', in People's Knowledge Editorial Collective (eds), *People's Knowledge and Participatory Action Research: Escaping the White-Walled Labyrinth*, pp. 113–134, Practical Action Publishing, Rugby <http://dx.doi.org/10.3362/9781780449395.012>.

About the authors

Hugh Kelly is the founding director of Swingbridge Media, which has been making films and video with people in the north-east of England for nearly 40 years. He has a website at www.swingbridgemedia.co.uk.

Graham Jeffery is reader in music and performance, and deputy director of the Culture & Creativity Research Hub at the University of the West of Scotland. He keeps a blog at www.generalpraxis.org.uk.

CHAPTER 8
A civil rights activist reflects on research

David Clay

Abstract

How can co-produced research, carried out on black people's terms, contribute to social justice? I describe the racial discrimination that black people encountered in the process of producing a local newsletter focusing on the history and experience of the black community in Liverpool, UK. Despite the obstacles, including the challenges to secure funding, I show how working together as a community can bring about a sense of ownership and shared goals. This snapshot of the 'black experience' during the time of the Toxteth riots in the 1980s is crafted through my experience as a civil rights activist and my reflections on institutionalized racism and social exclusion over 40 years.

Keywords: co-production, participatory research, social exclusion, racism, civil rights, Liverpool, Toxteth

Introduction

I was born in 1950 – the son of an African father and a white mother who'd spent most of her life in Liverpool.[1] I've never seen my dad. I was brought up without a father but with a very strong mother, because as you can imagine, in the 1950s and '60s we were brought up in poverty, without any doubt. But there was always a work ethic and an educational ethic from the family, and an idea that you had to make do yourself.

Words like 'social justice' and 'research' are words that have played a central role in my life. It would be useful to give my definition of both words from a grassroots, rather than an academic, perspective. This will enable the reader to understand the impact these words have had on many decisions that I have made.

Social justice. I consider such a term to be an indication of how you are treated in society, or for the purpose of this paper it is how you believe you are treated on the streets, in social situations, and as an individual. Your expectations are that you will be treated fairly and have the necessary apparatus to address any treatment that you consider unfair, and in the case of unfair treatment, be able to seek justice through the appropriate channels.

I didn't have too many role models from Liverpool. I basically turned to things, like a lot of lads like me did at the time. We turned to America and in many ways we imitated black America: the Black Panther Party. I knew about civil rights activists George Jackson and Bobby Seale, and *The Wretched of the Earth* by Frantz Fanon (1963). I'd read *Soul on Ice*; it was by Eldridge Cleaver

http://dx.doi.org/10.3362/9781780449395.009

(1968), an excellent book. And obviously that opened my eyes, because you've got to remember also when it was that I was at school, as a black Scouser: I mean, this was the age of Agatha Christie's *Ten Little Niggers*. There was no way of making you feel good and proud of yourself, or proud of your heritage, or proud of anything, because there was just nothing.

Research. This is a term that immediately suggests that in order to demonstrate a particular point or belief, you have to provide evidence that supports your 'theory'. In many instances an individual may prove a point with a minimum of input, and can carry out such research via a growing number of media. A 'researcher', on the other hand, has a specific role, and training, and can link with the appropriate 'organization' to uncover facts and opinions that endeavour to provide evidence to support a view or belief.

As a black person born in the city of Liverpool, 'social justice' is a term that I questioned from an early age, without actually being aware of its implications. Why, you first ask yourself, are you treated differently in certain situations? I often try and recall instances during my school days that highlighted this view. There are so many. There were areas in the city that black males or females went to at their own risk. In most cases, gangs were based on the colour of your skin and, to a large extent, your geographical location determined your experience (see Box 8.1).

I grew up in the area where we were known as 'shines', for obvious reasons. There was a joke at the time: Upper Parliament Street was 'the cleanest street in Liverpool' because there was a 'shine' on every corner. But we embraced that word. We described ourselves as 'shine boys'. So in many ways we were struggling with identity, without realizing we were struggling with identity.

Box 8.1 An example of social injustice

The Army and Navy stores in Liverpool: security had said that a young black lad had stolen a coat there. The lad had wanted to show the guard the label to demonstrate it was not stolen. The security guard had said 'No, you're not looking at that label'. The guard had ended up assaulting him, before finding out that it was the lad's own jacket. So the lad went to a solicitor and decided to complain to the store; the store wrote back and said they'd already investigated the matter and … 'bye bye'. So the lad came to the Black Organization and told us about his situation.

So a group of our people went to the Army and Navy stores at the peak hour on a Saturday morning at 11 o'clock. We were going to be spending, buying everything in half pences in order to cause a lot of inconvenience at the tills. The staff at the stores at the time wore red, and so all the females who came with us wore red just to confuse the situation. One group of us were just doing silly things like, you know, taking the laces out, or pretending to faint. And all the action we were taking was legal: it was legal to spend half pences, it was legal to ask for laces, it was legal to faint. So we were doing legal things, but causing the utmost disturbance and inconvenience to both shoppers and staff. Army and Navy stores eventually asked us what we wanted. We said 'Well, first of all, we are going be coming every Saturday morning, doing this kind of thing till we get what we want, which is basically an apology to the kid, and we want him to be reimbursed for the jacket.' Also, we knew that they had to declare themselves as an equal opportunities employer. And so the Army and Navy stores agreed to all the demands. Obviously, as you can imagine, that was not only a victory; it was also fun.

So when we pushed for Black Studies,[2] they said that was okay. You can have Black Studies, but you can have it every week on Upper Parliament Street, down in the cellar, so to speak, and so we never, I never got it ingrained. But what it did do was politicize us. Young girls who didn't know that they had a history found out that there were heroines as well as heroes.

It soon becomes evident that you are 'different'. In my case I was part of a so-called coloured population – the son or daughter of a mixed marriage. Despite the fact that you only spoke 'English', or in our case 'Scouse', you were still finding yourself a victim of your colour, even though you were born and bred in the city. On a legislative level, the 1965 Race Relations Act (Wikipedia, 2016) was introduced, which made it a civil offence to discriminate against people on the grounds of colour. Regardless of its actual impact, it was an admission that social justice was not working.

Shebeens were clubs that were part of our community's life, particularly in the 1940s. Because, in terms of social life, the blues (clubs) and shebeens were part of your community. You knew you could go to the blues, even at 2 in the morning, and just chill. Well, (later) all that was just outlawed. Yet they had been safe havens for local people.

In Toxteth, Liverpool, this 'coloured' community started to organize itself in the 1970s, in an effort to bring about social justice in education, in employment, and in society in general. In many ways we were a race that was not

Local protest against police brutality - Liverpool in the late 1960s

necessarily recognized, a part of Liverpool that found ourselves stereotyped and judged on the basis of pigmentation. Discrimination was quite evident to 'us', but who was going to believe us?

How could we show the lack of social justice?

There was only one route that would 'prove' our experience. That route was research. The 1970s onwards were to see individual, organizational, and governmental research demonstrating the lack of social justice for the Liverpool black community. It painted a picture that showed social exclusion in most aspects of social participation, from education to employment.[3]

I'm only going over this to give you a flavour of why 1981 was so ferocious. On an individual level, I had no love for the police any more than they had for me, but on the social and political level, like I said, the police proved themselves to be racist when the black community was being attacked. They'd done the same in 1945; they'd done the same in 1972; and then, as if that wasn't bad enough, in 1978, *The Listener* (a former BBC magazine which ceased publication in 1991) sent Martin Young to Liverpool to do an article on the hard work of the Merseyside police and how they dealt with violence and drunkenness. In the article, he spoke with the Merseyside police.

The gist of the story was that Merseyside police, and detectives in general, didn't have too many problems with black people, but that they did with the 'half-castes', who were products of black seamen and white prostitutes; had no natural home life; and were not considered to be black by blacks, and not considered to be white by whites. And so they had no life at all.

As you can see, the Merseyside police had already shown their colours on four occasions. So when 1981 came, there were a lot of old scores to settle, so to speak. Although it wasn't a race riot in the strictest sense of the word, it was a riot. It had racial elements in it. It started with black youth, and the fact that it involved people as young as 10 and 11, right through to people as old as 70, was a sign of the frustration that had built up.

I look back over 40 years of research and still the remnants of social exclusion exist. We have identified how institutionalized racism has ensured that we still have very little involvement in the economic progression in the city. We have no 'voice' that articulates our exclusion. It was this latter fact that encouraged me to try and create a medium that would, albeit at a parochial level, address this gap in our history and give the community a voice that will at least be heard, even if only within their own neighbourhood.

The *Granby Toxteth Review*

I was not new to creating written material that highlighted our exclusion, and working in a team setting. During my time employed by the Merseyside Community Relations Council, both as a 'Liverpool 8' (L8) fieldworker (working across the L8 area, which included Toxteth) and a public education officer, we established a resource centre dedicated to literature that concentrated on the Liverpool black experience. We linked up with schools and employers and produced newsletters, lectures, and equal opportunity courses. As assistant director of the Race Equality Unit at the Liverpool Education Department, we produced a magazine, *Race Equality News*.

Still the reality remained the same. So I decided to create my own magazine. It is relevant to outline how I went about turning this 'dream' into reality. In 2003, I sat with a number of friends and told them how I was going to produce a magazine that would have a Liverpool black perspective. I had called it the *Black Review*. Immediately the conversation turned to the dangers of using that title when hoping to attract funding. We had now been stripped of our identity and found ourselves within the category of 'ethnic minority'. I had to agree that the name might not be a good idea, and we discussed a more 'positive' approach. The name *Granby Toxteth Review* (GTR) seemed more sensible, as it depicted the location where most black people in the city lived. The Granby area was known throughout the country, as the 1981 riots had put Toxteth firmly on the map. The name was also less threatening to potential funders and it was agreed to be more appropriate for attracting sponsorship.

I should mention that, regarding racism in Liverpool, it's definitely got better. There isn't any doubt about that. A lot of barriers have been knocked down. I would like to think that they were economic and employment barriers, but they're not; they're social barriers. It's the recent increase in numbers of people from the European Union and other so-called immigrants that makes those white people who consider themselves the indigenous population say to black Scousers like me, 'Oh, you're a Scouse, you're one of us. Look at those Somalis, who are going to that school. My kid got kicked out' (though without saying why their child had lost their place). So the issue started to become less based on colour, so to speak, and more about length of residence. Regarding us, they now said, 'Well, you always have been Scouse and always have been from Liverpool, you know'. So we weren't the enemy any more. They even appear to forget there ever was racism against us. Their enemies are now cast as the Somalis, Poles, or Czechs.

Although I had never attempted to produce a magazine myself before, I prepared an outline of the contents. The objectives of the magazine were to focus on the history and social experience of the Liverpool-born black community. I carried out all the interviews and took all the photos. I decided that all articles should be substantiated with the appropriate research, and that they should simply present the facts and let the reader decide. This is why many of the articles ended with 'What do you think?'

Now that the format had been determined, I set off on the road to secure some financing. I immediately found myself in the funding maze. Funding organizations responded: 'you're just an individual', or 'you're not a registered charity', or 'you have no equal opportunities policy', or 'you have no bank account', or 'you have no constitution', or 'you have no management committee', or 'you have no annual accounts'. I received rejection after rejection.

I spent some time working with students from the Liverpool Community College who were on a journalism course, and I got acquainted with

QuarkXPress, a computer software programme I could use to produce the magazine. Initially the students started to work on the articles I prepared. But it transpired that they considered the material to be 'racist', since it only depicted the black experience in the city. I smiled to myself as I thought of how the local *Liverpool Echo* had no black journalists, and that black people only made it into the paper if it was to do with crime or sport. The reality was that I had to do the magazine myself.

I got my first sponsorship opportunity from the Arts Council based in Manchester, and was also the recipient of a contribution from the millionaire Sir John Moores. I had 2,000 copies of Issue 1 printed, with contributions from people all over the neighbourhood. Although the quality of the finished product was not high, I was over the moon about the contents. It was compiled entirely in my front room, on the most basic computer equipment. It would take at least four magazines before I would come to terms with the intricacies of magazine preparation.

The magazines went like hot cakes. They seemed to be everywhere in the community and people would ask 'When's the next one?' That was a good question. Where was I going to raise the finance for a second issue? I was eventually to produce eight magazines, with eight different sponsors, but that was all to come. Readers should be aware that I had no intention of making any profit from this venture. The magazine was to be free and produced on a quarterly basis. I decided to set up a subscription system, whereby I would ensure that customers received four magazines a year for a fee of £10. I gathered almost 400 subscribers.

I decided to rent an office. Within weeks I had three GTR staff, all Liverpool-born black, who agreed to work on a voluntary basis and strive to raise appropriate funding. I now had a team with similar aspirations to my own. They brought with them a wide range of skills and experience – photography, digital expertise, interview skills, administration, and research.

We had a journalistic approach. We had staff meetings with a set agenda. We established a major resource in the community. We took hundreds of photographs of local people and buildings, and conducted countless interviews. Not only had we fully equipped the office, we had also created a resource centre with an abundance of race-related materials for community and educational use. The team determined the content and we allocated tasks accordingly. I still took on the responsibility of editing and writing the final articles. We also had community members who agreed to contribute articles. Regular features were based on the expertise that we had available, and the desire to have articles that locals could relate to (see Box 8.2). This approach ensured local participation. All articles were produced with the full consent of the team, with no known dissent from the community.

The magazine generated a sense of community, as local people were eager to make contributions. The office was seen as a safe community haven, where people would drop in for coffee and share information that was relevant to the magazine.

BOX 8.2 Outline of regular contents for the *Granby Toxteth Review*

THE USUAL SUSPECTS: A few of the group went to the cinema on a regular basis so it was decided that they could be film critics

MRS. DOE FROM TOXTETH: An opportunity to comment on news heard on the radio

UNDERCOVER BROTHER: An opportunity for a 'third party' to comment on events from a grassroots viewpoint, without fear of identification

TOXTETH HALL OF FAME: Profiles of community members

TOXTETH PHOTO GALLERY: An opportunity to portray photographs of people in the community

---

GRANBY TOXTETH REVIEW

Front Cover: Carl John

Editorial 2

Toxteth TV: Passing Through or Serious Opportunities for our Youth ? 2

Crackhouse: The Reality 4

Refugees: Looking Through the Window of Racism 5

The Usual Suspects 7

Black History Month: The Bandwagon 9

African Music: Souad Massi 11

Liverpool Housing Trust 12

Toxteth Photo Gallery 14

Granby Elections: The New Girl in Town 15

Meet Mrs. Doe from Toxteth 17

The Toxteth Hall of Fame 18

Contacting the Granby Toxteth Review 18

Toxteth Kopite View: Spitting in the Wind 19

Undercover Brother: Does Rap Music Influence Gun Culture in Liverpool ? 20

Black Out Productions 22

Truth: Subscribe To The Granby Toxteth Review 22

Memories are Made of This Where Did All Our Clubs Go? 23

Competition: Win £25 (tokens) 23

Merseyside Caribbean Cricket Team 24

EDITORIAL

HAPPY BIRTHDAY GTR

Well we have survived our first year of publishing the Review. We would never have reached this milestone without the help and support of many individuals and local organisations. May we also thank the sponsors of our first four issues (see page 18), we hope that they may consider further support. A special mention to all those who subscribed to the Magazine during its first year - Nuff Respect. We continue to ensure that the magazine remains free of charge and consequently have to rely on fresh air and our own determination to create a viable grassroots publication.

HELP THE REVIEW HELP YOU

To all businesses and organisations! Have you considered the advertising potential of the GTR ? Let the community know about Job Vacancies, courses, events and products that you are offering. Get in touch with us for the most competitive rates. See Page 18.

SUBSCRIBE TODAY FOR AN INFORMED TOMORROW

TOXTETH TV: PASSING THROUGH OR SERIOUS OPPORTUNITIES FOR OUR YOUTH ?

Mission Hall in Windsor Street, Liverpool 8 - Original Headquarters of Toxteth TV

When you hear that a major project has arrived in the area and proceeds to purchase large chunks of property, it raises the question as to whether or not this is a programme that will bring some benefits for our young and talented. When the same Project attracts a £1.8 million capital input from the Government, claiming to be different, in that it has a focus on increased access for the under-represented, you start to wonder wey gots the scay gore?

As readers will be aware our own Mrs. Doe was sceptical and believed that action speaks louder than words. There is a visible under-representation of minority groups within the TV and Media industry, in Liverpool, and it was this that took us inquiringly to the doors of Toxteth TV.

2

Cover of Issue 1 of the *Granby Toxteth Review*

The *Granby Toxteth Review* editorial team at work (from a drawing published in the GTR)

The *Granby Toxteth Review* highlighted how a local initiative made a community feel able to articulate its own beliefs, and many saw the publication as an opportunity to get involved with 'community politics'.

Challenges to secure funding

As an outcome of years of research and riots, an increasing number of agencies became the recipients of funding earmarked for the development of the Toxteth community. The city received millions of pounds of European funding, channelled through such programmes as the Single Regeneration Budget and the Toxteth Task Force, set up by the former Environment Minister, Michael Heseltine. There were also a growing number of government-aided schemes. Despite all the funding, there was little change to the lives of local people, although some benefited from short-term work offered by these projects as they 'passed through'.

Throughout this period, the *Granby Toxteth Review* acted as a voice that scrutinized every development. This was to culminate in the inventive *Social Exclusion Game*, created by the GTR team. The board game depicted the maze of agencies that had descended on the area. It illustrated the obstacles that local people had to overcome if they wanted to receive any financial help.

These observations were not welcomed by the 'powers that be' and we won few friends within the major funding circles. The Government Office of Liverpool, for example, offered us a £2,460 grant on the condition that we refrained from making derogatory comments about the government agencies. These conditions were not imposed on other groups. We refused their offer, albeit to our own financial detriment.

We still managed to raise funding to produce seven editions of the GTR on a quarterly basis, with seven different sponsors and a growing number of subscribers. However, with each publication costing £2,000, we were struggling to meet the running costs.

It soon became more and more difficult to raise the funding to continue the magazine and, after Issue 7, we had little choice but to stop. We had not been able to publish Issue 8 and I felt that I had let a lot of people down, in particular our subscribers. I was fortunate that two or three years later I was able to publish Issue 8, thanks to support from a small local fund called the Austin Smith Memorial Small Grants Fund, set up in memory of a priest and community activist who dedicated his time to serving the local community and tackling racism.

I have sons and daughters of my own and hopefully we've done enough for them to feel proud of who they are. Liverpool's black community has been unlucky in many ways. We've had a generation of people who will shoot their own people for the sake of a tenner, or for standing on someone's foot by accident, or for other petty things like that, or in drug wars. A lot is being lost in the mix.

The value of co-produced research

I am in no doubt that without the co-produced research that people like me undertake, many communities, like Toxteth, would find difficulty in having their issues addressed. Research is essential in bringing the issues to the attention of the relevant agencies, although there is no guarantee that any action will be taken. Once the level of deprivation in Toxteth had been identified, the city became a major target for government funding and there was a huge amount of research carried out over many years. Research carried out following the Stephen Lawrence case (see Singh, 2016) highlighted the institutional racism in the Metropolitan Police Force, but did not necessarily end such racism. It is a difficult task for most researchers to achieve social justice within communities that have experienced countless years of injustice.

There are, however, many instances where joint research is beneficial. One would be where the link with established 'community bodies' strengthens the researchers' established goals. Working with 'professional' bodies such as a university also adds weight to research. The only alternative to this is communities working alone. This is difficult owing to the apathy of many community members who feel that nothing will change. History has shown us that once an issue has been identified via research there is always a reaction, be it positive or negative.

In any case, for any co-produced research to be successful, there has to be initial empathy from the researchers, which in turn brings about a confidence in the community that things can happen. From experience, many researchers see no further than getting the job done and leaving the situation as quickly as they arrived, regardless of what impact it may have, or not, on social justice.

I'm now a performer. I'm an artist, I'm a singer, and I enjoy doing gigs. Where I wouldn't particularly relish walking through Huyton at 12:30 at night by myself, I'd have no problem whatsoever about being in a venue in Huyton at 12:30 at night, because music would be the winner there, so to speak. And you'd be seen for what talent you had, rather than for the colour of your skin.

Hopefully the days when researchers have little to no empathy with the people they link up with are well and truly in the past. Personally I used to dwell on the 'class' and 'race' gap, and found it difficult to comprehend that a middle-class researcher could come to Toxteth and understand the feelings and pain that the community has experienced over countless years. I now know that gap is being addressed.

My story of the *Granby Toxteth Review* shows how working together as a community can bring about a sense of ownership and shared goals. If we had had the support of academic researchers, who knows how far we might have progressed? There is little doubt that co-produced research is a powerful tool in bringing about social justice within communities that have little to no power or voice with which to articulate their own frustration or need.

Notes

1. See Wakeford (2012) for an animated video illustrating sections of an interview with David Clay on some of the themes of this chapter.
2. Black Studies is the study of the histories, politics, and cultures of black peoples of the world.
3. See the Liverpool Black Experience (2016), an online community documenting the history of black people in Liverpool from a grassroots perspective.

References

Cleaver, E. (1968) *Soul on Ice*, Ramparts Press, San Francisco, CA.

Fanon, F. (1963) *The Wretched of the Earth*, Grove Press, New York, NY.

Liverpool Black Experience (2016) <https://www.facebook.com/Liverpool-Black-Experience-218540358158> [accessed 9 August 2016].

Singh, J. (2016) 'Cultivating an anti-racist position in post-race society', in People's Knowledge Editorial Collective (eds), *People's Knowledge and Participatory Action Research: Escaping the White-Walled Labyrinth*, pp. 47–54, Practical Action Publishing, Rugby <http://dx.doi.org/10.3362/9781780449395.005>.

Wakeford, T. (2012) *A Short Film about Dave Clay* [film]. Available at: <https:// vimeo. com/37491854> [accessed 25 August 2016].

Wakeford, T. (2012) A Short Film about Dave Clay [film]. Available at: <https:// vimeo. com/37491854> [accessed 25 August 2016].

Wikipedia (2016) 'Race Relations Act 1965' <https://en.wikipedia.org/wiki/Race_Relations_Act_1965> [accessed 9 August 2016].

About the author

David Clay has a degree in sociology. He was formerly the assistant director of race equality at Liverpool City Council and later worked for the British Science Association. He is based in Liverpool, where he works as a singer.

CHAPTER 9

LIVErNORTH: combining individual and collective patient knowledge

Tilly Hale

Abstract

Who are the 'experts' when it comes to patient care and medical research? Patient knowledge, both individually and collectively, is showing signs of slowly but surely becoming respected and valued by the medical profession. Despite the difficulties and frustrations encountered when making one's voice heard in a room full of 'experts', my involvement in medical research as a patient with liver disease and in setting up a patient participation group at a hospital in Newcastle in north-east England, shows the progress that can be made when health researchers recognize the expertise of patients living with chronic disease.

Keywords: patient and public involvement (PPI), participatory research, patient groups, expert patients, liver disease

Background

This is the story of how I became a patient and, after a long time, had my knowledge recognized by professional researchers to the benefit of myself and others. I used to be a healthy woman who was a single parent to two children. I regularly played badminton and squash, enjoyed dog walking, and was a Brownie Guide leader. I had a good social life and generally was very active.

In 1985, having just turned 40, I began to feel tired and have 'aches and pains'. I saw my GP as I wondered if I had arthritis – my hands were very painful and I found decorating difficult, although I had always been able to look after the upkeep of my home. He agreed that it might be arthritis and started to treat me. However, six months on he decided to carry out some blood tests. The first tests came back in November; however, he told me that the laboratories had 'messed up' and that he would have to repeat the tests, which he did, and asked me to return after the beginning of the year.

When I returned, he told me I had a rare disease called primary biliary cirrhosis (PBC), an auto-immune liver disease, and that I probably had only a year or so to live. He immediately referred me to the Freeman Hospital in Newcastle in the north-east of England, which was local to me, and my first appointment was two weeks later. I learned that PBC mainly affects women – with

http://dx.doi.org/10.3362/9781780449395.010

the ratio of nine women to one man – and that it was more common in the north-east of England than anywhere else. On my first visit to the hospital I was told that I probably had at least five years to live, and that my GP would have only known of the disease from post-mortems, which would account for him thinking I might only have a year. At this stage I had no tests other than the blood tests. As my daughter was 17 and my son was 13, I was concerned that I might die whilst they were still very young. The tiredness was increasing and looking after my children was proving very difficult – they were mainly being fed on takeaways and although clothes were being washed regularly, ironing was a problem – usually it was a shirt each for the next day, with my own clothes becoming strangers to the iron.

In the following month I had a variety of tests, including a biopsy which placed me at Stage 1, the early stage of a four-stage disease. On this occasion, the same doctor told me I had between two and 20 years to live. I was not happy at the two and pointed out that a month before he had said I had at least five years. He replied that he had said two, but had also said up to 20 years. I was not happy with his attitude and told him that whilst I would return to the hospital as directed, I did not want to see him again.

Following that I went on to see a doctor who was much more on my wavelength, and I felt very comfortable with her. Unfortunately, she moved to a district hospital within a year or so and after that I saw a variety of senior registrars who had a range of attitudes towards my questions. Some were very good and talked to me and tried to explain what was going on. Because PBC was a rare disease, there was no form of support group and it was difficult to know how to meet up with other patients with this problem. Sadly, some of the doctors were very much of the mindset that they were the doctors and I was the patient, and they would look after me and I should not worry about it. I found this attitude very condescending and unhelpful.

One doctor told me that he had several patients who played tennis and squash on a regular basis and took part in lots of activities. I explained to him that I had always been active until a year or so before this, when I had started to feel very tired and also to have the aches and pains, but he gave me the impression that he thought I was lazy and that it was partly in my mind, which I found very upsetting. I left the hospital feeling very tearful and that I had to push myself to be more active. Fortunately, when I saw the next registrar and mentioned his colleague's comments, he told me that fatigue was one of the main problems of my disease, and of several liver diseases. He said I should try to introduce rest periods into my day. To be honest, I was so tired that a lot of the day was spent resting, in between dragging myself around doing minimum housework and grocery shopping. My social life had come to a halt, and as soon as my children were in bed, I too was off to bed.

Over the next few years, I visited the hospital every six months or so. I was always told that there was no treatment and no cure, and that they did not know the cause of the disease, but that they would look after me. I was grateful that I was in the hospital system and that I was being seen in a liver unit, as so many hospitals (especially district hospitals) do not have hepatologists on their staff, and so patients only see gastroenterologists. At the beginning there was very little research being carried out on PBC, although I was always keen to take part in any project and was occasionally included in studies for general liver diseases. However, it was rare to hear any results from the studies. There was still no known cause and no known cure.

In 1993, my bloods had deteriorated and I had a second biopsy. I was told that I was now Stage 4, which meant that my liver was cirrhotic. The good news was that there was now a transplant programme at the Freeman Hospital in Newcastle upon Tyne, and it was mentioned that this might be the path the health service would take with me.

Participating in research

In October 1993, a doctor spoke to me about a study she was conducting and asked if I would be willing to take part. I was only too keen. I began the study at the beginning of December 1993, as Patient No. 2. The study involved me going to the Freeman Hospital every day for 21 days, sometimes being there for just a few hours, other times being there for the whole day, and having a variety of procedures. Some of these were not very pleasant, but I was only too happy to be involved in a study where the doctor was working with a drug company. I responded very well to this study, unlike many of the other participants, to the extent that I was kept on the treatment long after the end of the trial. I had a new lease of life, was much more active, and felt more like my old self.

In February 1994, Professor Oliver James, head of the liver unit at the Freeman Hospital and Newcastle University, invited all of his liver patients to attend a meeting at the Freeman, with over 100 patients attending. Apart from the patients, the meeting was attended by Professor James, Professor Maggie Bassendine, Pam Buckley (the transplant coordinator), and Alison Rodgers of the British Liver Trust. Professor James was keen that patients should set up a support group and said he would do what he could to help us, but that we would be responsible for the running of any such group. A second meeting was arranged where 20 people turned up – these were people who were willing to help to get the group going. The meeting was run by Pam Buckley, who already knew me through my work as a chaplaincy lay visitor to the kidney unit, and she asked me if I would consider taking on the role of secretary. Although I was somewhat reluctant, I agreed to do this as I realized I had good knowledge of how such a group would operate and I had the required skills.

A committee was formed at that meeting consisting of a chairman, treasurer, myself as secretary, and two other people who were keen to be involved at that level. We set about forming the group, which became known as LIVErNORTH (see Box 9.1), and organized a general meeting with a speaker from the liver unit who was willing to attend and talk about liver disease in general.

Box 9.1 LIVErNORTH

'LIVErNORTH is a national patient support group for adults with liver disease. It is based at the Freeman Hospital in Newcastle upon Tyne, UK.
LIVErNORTH is run entirely by unpaid volunteers and all of our services (including a helpline, newsletter and meetings) are absolutely free to UK liver patients, their carers and families. LIVErNORTH also funds research into all liver disease, and advocates for and supports the involvement of liver patients in relevant research, services and policy decision making.'

Source: LIVErNORTH, 2016

I finally felt that I was moving forward and gaining knowledge of my disease and other liver diseases. As a committee, we were very keen to invite the medical staff to give talks and be willing to answer questions that we might have or that might be raised by other patients, and we were also very keen to fundraise to help with amenities for the unit and research projects carried out with the university. The fact that the Freeman now had a transplant programme meant that many people were keen to be involved and to have a support group, not just for the patients but also for their families.

Over the next few years, LIVErNORTH grew in numbers and our finances were constantly improving. We had various fundraising events and many people raised money for us, which was very edifying. We had a newsletter, a variety of general meetings throughout the year, and also some social events, including a Christmas carol service and Christmas dinner, and an annual autumn fair.

The staff were pleased with our enthusiasm and began to involve us more and more in research studies. For the first time they also began to feed back the results of such studies – this was usually by coming to a meeting and talking to us about the project, which we found very interesting and which motivated us more and more to push for research to be carried out.

I was lucky in that I had several doctors who talked to me at length about my particular disease, and who were keen for me to learn more about it, spread the word amongst other patients, and to speak to medical people about the disease from a patient's perspective. I was always happy to do this, as I had realized that whilst the doctors knew about our diseases from the textbook point of view, it was the patients who knew what it was like to live with those diseases.

Around 1996, I had another change of doctor – Dr David Jones (now Professor). David had a very strong interest in PBC and was very keen to have patients involved in his studies. He encouraged me to talk to patients and try to show them the benefits of taking part in studies, not just for the doctors' sakes, but also for their own sakes, and for the sake of future patients. He and I formed a good working relationship, and thanks to him I began to learn more and more about my disease and about the problems the doctors had in trying to find answers.

Under the LIVErNORTH umbrella, David and I began to hold separate meetings which were PBC-specific. These were held at various hospitals throughout the northern region – Freeman, Sunderland Royal, Middlesbrough General, Bishop Auckland General, and Darlington General. In the early days, most of the talks were given by David, although a few other doctors did speak occasionally. These meetings generated a lot of interest in research projects, with patients agreeing to come to Newcastle to take part in various studies carried out by David and his colleague, Dr Julia Newton (now Professor). Julia had a background in geriatric medicine and was originally based at the Falls and Syncope Department of Newcastle University. Her knowledge of orthostatic problems (blood pressure, dizziness, etc.) and autonomic dysfunction were very useful in moving forward the understanding of why various problems occurred in PBC.

In July 1999, I had a liver transplant operation which went very well. I was in hospital for 17 days and then had a three-month recovery period at home. After this it was back to LIVErNORTH with more knowledge and more experience. This gave me another string to my bow, in that I had, as David Jones put it, gone from A–Z pre-transplant, and now had come through the operation very successfully.

Fatigue was now officially recognized as a problem in PBC, and cognitive impairment began to be studied. I was fortunate in that the team included me in getting volunteers to take part in many studies. Although these took place mostly at Newcastle University, on one occasion 20 patients and a team of doctors travelled to Hammersmith Hospital in London, where we had MRI scans on our brains.

Of course we still met opposition from various doctors who queried the fatigue and the cognitive problems and felt that the patients were imagining some of the symptoms. Sadly, this continues to this day, despite many papers written to prove otherwise.

I am now classed as an expert patient – of course I do not really see myself that way, but as David Jones says, he can tell doctors all about the disease but I can tell them about living with it. I have given numerous talks to various medical groups on the patient perspective, I have had an article produced in the *British Medical Journal* (Hale et al., 2012), and I have given a TEDx talk at Newcastle University (Hale, 2014). I have also been on the committee for the Research for Patient Benefit North East, looking at funding requests for various medical projects, and I am on several committees through Newcastle University Liver Department. Along with one of my colleagues, I am on a diagnostic evidence committee for Leeds University, and we are on the NHS Blood and Transplant lay committee looking at donor usage throughout the UK.

At Newcastle University there is a department called the LIVErNORTH Research Laboratory which was funded by our group. Over the 20 years of our existence, we have grown into a well-recognized patient support group, which also supports medical research and researchers.

In 2013 the UK-PBC Consortium was set up and received a £6 million grant to look at the disease; and I am a member of the steering committee. We now have several research projects underway looking into PBC, which is marvellous – in the past we only had one project at a time, and often nothing for quite a lot of the time. We now have drug companies actively interested in the disease, both British and American, and this is very encouraging.

Things have changed very much from the early days of my diagnosis – now patients are kept well informed about their disease, we are treated as part of the team, rather than just being bodies who are there to donate blood or complete questionnaires, and this makes patients feel valued and more willing to take part in research. Of course there are still doctors and hospital liver units where the old ways continue, but fortunately this is changing and patients now feel they have a voice and are more willing to use it. We feel the studies carried out today may not benefit some of us, owing to age etc., but we are hopeful that they will help people who are coming behind us. When I was first diagnosed, there was a three-line item in the Encyclopaedia Britannica saying that PBC mainly affected woman aged 55 and over. Now we know that it can affect women much younger than that and thankfully they are being diagnosed at an earlier age, so that whilst there is still no cure, at least they are given whatever treatments are available. Whilst many people have still never heard of PBC, they can now find out a great deal about it once they are diagnosed, and can realize that it is not a death sentence. A lot of work is being done on trying to improve the quality of life of patients with PBC and this alone would make living with the disease so much easier for patients and their families.

I feel very fortunate that I met Professor David Jones and Professor Julia Newton and that they included me in so much of their work. Their enlightened attitude towards patient involvement has made a huge difference to the way patients are included in projects and how patients are respected and valued. This concept is now spreading through many hospitals and medical schools and can only lead to improvements in treatments and patient care.

Reflections

Having my knowledge and experience recognized means a great deal to me. When I was first diagnosed, doctors were very kind, but they definitely saw me just as a patient, with no ideas of my own, and no real knowledge of the disease. Over the years, I gained a great deal of knowledge and obviously I became experienced in various tests such as biopsy, endoscopy, MRI scans, etc., not to mention the never-ending blood tests which were a routine part of every hospital appointment. Once I became involved with Professor Jones, I was given much more information about the disease and how he hoped to progress with finding answers. We often talked about possible causes, how research could move forward, and how patients could become more engaged in taking part in research. Because of my experience and knowledge, I was able to talk to other patients about the value of taking part in studies, and encourage them to take part. Many people do not realize that studies need significant numbers of patients and tend to think they do not need to be part of the research. I explain to them that if the research does not get the numbers, then the study will often fail and the drug companies will lose interest. A disease such as PBC, which is still significantly rare, does not attract the research that more common illnesses generate. Of all the major transplant programmes (heart, kidney, and liver), liver is the least well regarded. Sadly, the general public (and indeed the patients themselves) often regard liver disease as self-inflicted. Because my disease is auto-immune and because I am now almost 16 years post-transplant, I can show the positive face of liver disease and liver transplant. As a member of the UK-PBC Consortium steering committee, I come into contact with various pharmaceutical companies which are interested in my disease and how it has affected my life. The fact that my daughter has PBC also makes me very interesting to these companies because we are in the small percentage where the disease is familial. David Jones' backing of me, and the fact that he includes me in so many meetings, means that other doctors speak to me and ask my opinion, and drug companies also take my comments on board and are interested in my ideas.

The fact that other doctors recognize my knowledge and experience of PBC is very useful to other liver patients. When people are first diagnosed with this disease it is very rare for them to have heard of it. Usually, with the name primary biliary cirrhosis, the only word they understand (or think they understand) is cirrhosis, and often they comment that they do not drink very much alcohol at all. As another patient, I am often asked to speak to them and can reassure them that all cirrhosis means is 'scarring' – sadly for most people the word signifies alcoholism, which is completely incorrect. Early in my diagnosis I was told by Professor Oliver James, the then head of the Freeman Liver Unit and Head of the Newcastle University Liver Unit, that you could have 100 people standing at the bar – 100 men or 100 women, the same size and build, drinking the same drinks. One or maybe two people could go on to develop alcohol-related liver disease; the other 98 or 99 would have no problems with their livers. For people being told they need a liver transplant, I am able to reassure them that it is not the end of the world. I can tell them what I have achieved in the years since my transplant (two half marathons – fast walked, but completed; four visits to the Transplant Games where I took part in a variety of sports; and generally living a very enjoyable life). This is not only helpful for the patients but for their families, who see an active (admittedly elderly) woman who is certainly not sitting around being a victim or even seeing herself as a patient (despite all the tablets).

When I was first diagnosed, the term 'patient and public involvement' (PPI) was unknown. Patients were not involved – they were patients, they would be looked after, they would be treated kindly, but they would not be *involved*. Some doctors took the view that patients did not need to know their results; these could be left to the doctor to know – he or she would look after the patient and all the patient needed to do was attend clinic, give blood, and go home. Over the years, a much more enlightened attitude has emerged where doctors realize the value of involving patients. To date, this takes many forms.

Patients are invited to be on steering committees for drug trials – this allows them to give their opinions on how trials are to be run, whether the trial is suitable for patients, or whether the trials are too extreme (as in the number of hospital visits involved, numbers of questionnaires to be completed etc., and also making any such items patient-friendly). Patients are often involved on ethics committees, on research for patient benefit committees (where researchers apply for funding for their projects), and in helping to produce patient information sheets etc., as well as actually taking part in the projects. We now have workshops dealing with patient involvement, and these are very well attended by patients who are very keen to be involved in any aspect that is open to them.

Unfortunately, there are still many hospitals where this is not the norm, where there is mainly a degree of tokenism, and patients are very much left in the dark about many aspects of their disease and indeed their care! I would like to see ways in which all patients are given the opportunity to be involved in their treatment, where their opinions are valued, and where they are made to feel that they can make suggestions on research topics. I know of several pieces of PBC research that have come about through patients talking about their problems, and where their doctors have listened to them and thought about their comments. I have been very fortunate in that Professor David Jones has always included me in his work, but I know this is not true of all hospitals – if the day ever comes when it is normal, I think research will go forward in great leaps. After all, patients are the people who have the disease; they are the ones who live with it every day, and find ways of coping with the difficulties of their disease and the effect it has on them and their families and friends. Doctors may know this in their heads, but they definitely do not know it through living with diseases. Patients know it, though, and no matter how well or how poorly educated they are, they have ideas about why things happen, and certainly they have ideas on how to cope with the problems. If doctors would listen to these comments and give them some thought, they might indeed come up with some answers to various 'mysteries' of the diseases. If patients are made to feel their ideas are useful, then they will be more willing to speak out about how they perceive their illnesses, and who knows, one of these days answers may be found through a joint effort of doctors and patients.

References

Hale, M. Newton, J.L. and Jones, D.E.J. (2012) 'Fatigue in primary biliary cirrhosis', British Medical Journal 2012; 345: e7004 <http://dx.doi.org/10.1136/bmj.e7004>.

Hale, M. (2014) 'A patient perspective', TEDx Talk at Newcastle University, June TEDxNewcastle [video], <https://www.youtube.com/watch?v=v1Ml1djOyB8> [accessed 9 August 2016].

LIVErNORTH (2016) <http://www.livernorth.org.uk/> [accessed 9 August 2016].

About the author

Tilly Hale co-founded LIVErNORTH, a national patient support group for adults with liver disease. Tragically she died of cancer during the production stages of this book. A tribute to her in the Spring 2016 edition of LIVErNEWS can be downloaded from <http://www.livernorth.org.uk/pdfs/ln53.pdf>.

CHAPTER 10

The original citizen scientists

People's Knowledge Editorial Collective with paintings from Haiti by Michel Lafleur

Abstract

What can we learn from history about the importance of non-dominant groups in society participating in citizen science? This picture essay from Haiti is a response to the increasing use of the term 'citizen scientist' to describe researchers who lack professional training in science. The historical significance of public participation in scientific research is illustrated by the role that white European scientists played during the colonial period in preventing Haitians attaining their basic rights to life. We acknowledge the expertise of people of colour, including those from peasant backgrounds in the Global South, in the pursuit of universal human rights and social justice. We also discuss how the term 'citizen science' risks further entrenching scientism, and challenge the notion that physics-based science is the only authoritative way of understanding and interpreting the world. The different goals, questions, and methods involved in different research traditions must be acknowledged.

Keywords: citizen science, public participation in science, Haiti, scientism, cultural imperialism

The paintings that illustrate this chapter are by the Haitian artist Michel Lafleur. Photographs of the paintings were first exhibited at the inaugural conference of the Citizen Science Association at the 2015 Annual Meeting of the American Association for the Advancement of Science, San Jose, USA.[1] The 600 delegates at the conference came from 25 countries, yet 90–95 per cent appeared to be white and of European descent. Our exhibit was called *Who are the citizen scientists?* We wanted to show the diversity of people, from the history of a single nation, who might be what universities are increasingly calling 'citizen scientists'.

Citizen science (defined in the Glossary) is often used in connection with public participation in scientific research. It has been characterized in the media as a cure for societal and environmental problems and has become popular in some scientific circles.

The exhibit highlighted the fact that people of colour, including those from peasant backgrounds in the Global South (see Glossary), along with members of other non-dominant groups in society, should be considered just as capable of thinking scientifically as those with professional training. This observation

http://dx.doi.org/10.3362/9781780449395.011

Charlemagne Peralte, leader of the Cacos rebellion against the American invasion of Haiti in 1915. From traditional poster, 2015. Original painting by Michel Lafleur

Peasant woman collecting tree roots for making charcoal, Baille Tourib, Artibonite, Haiti. From photograph by Leah Gordon, 2015. Original painting by Michel Lafleur

is all the more poignant when we understand the role that white European scientists played during the European colonialist period in preventing Haitians attaining their basic rights to life.

Saint Domingue, as Haiti was called during its century of French rule, was the single richest and most productive colony in the world. The application of science, funded by powerful European traders, turned the land into plantations where imported slaves were transformed into brutalized mechanisms of profit for Europe's white elites – *les hauts blancs* (literally 'the top whites').

The exports of sugar and coffee from Haiti produced more wealth for France in 1776 than the whole of the Spanish empire in the Americas produced for Spain that year. This was a country the size of the tiny US state of Massachusetts and less than half the size of Wales.

The suffering in Haiti under this scientifically streamlined system of slavery was on a scale that we can hardly imagine. At least a million slaves died prematurely, with many thousands choosing suicide instead. Amidst this slaughter, scientists drawn from the *hauts blancs* established a Royal Society of Sciences and Arts in the colony.

Claudel Casseus, ghetto author from the Grand Rue neighbourhood, Port-au-Prince, Haiti.
Photograph by Adler Pierre, 2015. Original painting by Michel Lafleur

Fishing boat off the shores of Leogane, Haiti. From photograph by Leah Gordon, 2015. Original painting by Michel Lafleur

Maurice Semilos, carpenter and furniture maker from Ghetto Leanne, Grand Rue, Port-au-Prince, Haiti. Photograph by Claudel Casseus, 2015. Original painting by Michel Lafleur

Joseph Ducaste, Tap Tap driver and mechanic, from the Grand Rue neighbourhood, Port-au-Prince, Haiti. From photograph by Claudel Casseus, 2015. Original painting by Michel Lafleur

Faced with stirrings of slave revolt, the August 1791 meeting of the society's 160 members decided to add 'political science' to its range of interests. For these *hauts blancs*, the best way to deal with these upheavals was more scientific analysis. But their scientific imagination proved to be fatally flawed. Six days after their meeting, 100,000 slaves rose up and destroyed plantations across the north of the territory. Within 10 days, thousands of *hauts blancs*, presumably including many members of its Royal Society, had been killed. By 1804, the Haitian revolutionaries were triumphant. They avenged their oppressors by massacring almost every last remaining white person in Haiti, and tearing the colour white out of the French Tricolour – leaving the red and blue flag that Haitians still use today.

Two hundred years ago, Haiti was the only nation in which slaves had successfully won their freedom. Fifteen years after France's 1789 Declaration of the Rights of Man and of the Citizen,[2] Haiti's successful and

Peasant coffee producer in Cayes Jacmel, Haiti. From photograph by Leah Gordon, 2015. Original painting by Michel Lafleur

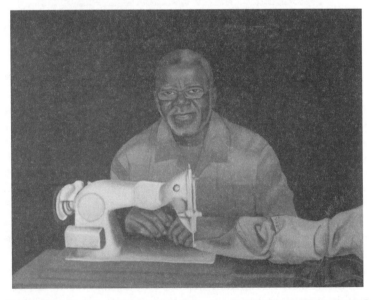

Boss Thelius Simeon, independent tailor off Boulevard Jean-Jacques Dessalines, Port-au-Prince, Haiti. From photograph by Leah Gordon, 2015. Original painting by Michel Lafleur

Rara band in Jacmel, Haiti. From photograph by Richard Fleming, 2015. Original painting by Michel Lafleur

bloody uprising dispatched the slaves' colonial masters back to Europe. They had refused to be subject to a declaration that condemned black people to be colonial slaves, and that allowed white people to appoint themselves as the only citizens, in that no-one else could have basic human rights.

The *hauts blancs'* vision of science was an early form of scientism (see Glossary). Lawrence Krauss, a cosmologist at Arizona State University, has laid out the key principles of scientism (see Box 10.1). It was not surprising that the Royal Society of Saint Domingue converted a political problem about human dignity, freedom, and justice into one of science.

The term citizen science risks further entrenching scientism, unless we challenge the notion that physics-based science is the only authoritative way of understanding and interpreting the world. We need a greater appreciation of the different goals, questions, and methods involved in different research traditions (see Table 10.1).

Box 10.1 The key principles of scientism

1. All questions are either meaningless or can be answered by physical science.
2. Science has authority because it is based on empirical evidence. Factual claims made by physical science will therefore always overrule other claims.
3. Physical science provides the ultimate account of the basis of reality but it substantively changes the questions, getting to the correct ones, rather than the meaningless ones that are posed by non-scientists.

Summarised from: Krauss, 2014

Table 10.1 How different worldviews inform approaches to research

Worldview/ aspect	Physical/quantitative science	Qualitative/artistic inquiry	Doing hybrid research inclusively
Goals	Discovering universal truths; scaling up to larger areas or populations; predicting future states of the world; controlling behaviour	Unravelling of accepted truths; construction of personal truths; exploration of the specific; generation of art	Constructing situated knowledges; troubling the taken-for-granted; pragmatic guidance for practitioners
Questions	What does it mean from the researcher's point of view? What is the relationship among factors? What behaviours can be predicted?	How do/can we cope with life? What other ways can we imagine? What is unique about my or another's experience?	How do participants understand their world? How can we co-construct a different world? What are the practical implications of our work?
Methods	Coding and measuring; random sampling; frequencies of behaviours; surveys; structured interviews	Dialogue; performance; introspection; visual arts; storytelling	Discussion groups; grounded theory; participatory action research; collective historical/archival research

Adapted from: Ellingson, 2011

As it excludes of all knowledge apart from that generated by physical/ quantitative science, scientism has been exposed by a range of thinkers as narrow-minded nonsense, most notably by moral philosopher Mary Midgley.[3] In a lecture entitled 'Science, scientism and the self', Midgley (2015) showed how scientism arose and is maintained by the dominance of physics and individualism in Western thinking. Under neoliberalism (see Glossary), it is still commonly accepted in scientific institutions and corporate boardrooms across the world. The days of overt colonialism may be in the past, but scientism has underpinned the concept of the 'selfish gene', a gene-centred view of evolution, which has been key to providing scientific justification for the neo-colonial project of globalization.

The challenge for those who promote citizen science is to show that they have learned from science's colonial and more recent neocolonial history. We need to harness action-orientated, hybrid modes of research that are carried out inclusively (see right column of Table 10.1), such as participatory action research, alongside other approaches learned from other social movements (see 'Signposts for people's knowledge', Wakeford, 2016). We believe that together we can build alliances for a more inclusive knowledge system and vision for the future than the one being created and sustained by institutions run according to purely capitalist logics, including universities, non-governmental organizations and, most of all, corporations. If we can't, can we really call ourselves ethical researchers or responsible citizens?

Bebe, chef and restaurateur, 'Soutie Bon Griot' restaurant in Montrouis, Haiti. From photograph by Leah Gordon, 2015. Original painting by Michel Lafleur

Notes

1. For more information see Citizen Science Association (n.d.) and American Association for the Advancement of Science (2016).
2. For more information on France's 1789 Declaration of the Rights of Man and of the Citizen see Wikipedia (2016a).
3. For more information on Mary Midgley, see Wikipedia (2016b).

References

American Association for the Advancement of Science (2015) 'Annual Meeting 2015 Newsroom', <www.aaas.org/am2015-newsroom> [accessed 10 August 2016].

Citizen Science Association (no date) 'The power of citizen science', <http://citizenscienceassociation.org> [accessed 10 August 2016].

Ellingson, L. (2011) 'Analysis and representation across the continuum,' in N.K. Denzin and Y.S. Lincoln (eds), *The SAGE Handbook of Qualitative Research*, pp. 595–610, Sage Publications, Thousand Oaks, CA.

Krauss, L. (2014) 'Scientism and empirical evidence' [video], Panel discussion by Lawrence Krauss, <www.youtube.com/watch?v=jA-CPimg6WY> [accessed 10 August 2016].

Midgley, M. (2015) 'Science, scientism and the self' [video], Lecture delivered at the Ian Ramsey Centre – Humane Philosophy Project 2014–2015 Seminar, <https://www.youtube.com/watch?v=ekp1hEjtPsQ> [accessed 10 August 2016].

Wakeford, T. (2016) 'Signposts for people's knowledge', in People's Knowledge Editorial Collective (eds), *People's Knowledge and Participatory Action Research: Escaping the White-Walled Labyrinth*, pp. 113–134, Practical Action Publishing, Rugby <http://dx.doi.org/10.3362/9781780449395.012>.

Wikipedia (2016a) 'Declaration of the Rights of Man and of the Citizen', <https://en.wikipedia.org/wiki/Declaration_of_the_Rights_of_Man_and_of_the_Citizen> [accessed 10 August 2016].

Wikipedia (2016b) 'Mary Midgley', <https://en.wikipedia.org/wiki/Mary_Midgley> [accessed 10 August 2016].

About the authors

The People's Knowledge Editorial Collective jointly authored this chapter. They are **Nicole Kenton, Hinda Mohamed Smith, Chris Nelson, Javier Sanchez Rodriguez**, and **Tom Wakeford**.

About the artist

Michel Lafleur is a Haitian artist based at Manou Studio, Port-au-Prince, Haiti.

CHAPTER 11

Signposts for people's knowledge

Tom Wakeford

Abstract

How can we make sense of the mass of jargon that surrounds participatory action research? I look at three critical traditions of research as a lens through which to examine some of the theories and approaches covered in People's Knowledge and Participatory Action Research, *and provide signposts to navigate the territory we define as 'people's knowledge'. I describe the practice of citizens' juries, and show how to strengthen our understanding of the practice through a process of bricolage and then reflection on each individual jury. I also demonstrate that the practice of people's knowledge has as much to learn from art as it does from methodological novelty, and explore the ethics of participatory processes. As a postscript, I reflect on 25 years of work on social justice, environmental concerns, and the generation of knowledge.*

Keywords: people's knowledge, participatory action research, bricolage, citizens' jury, ethics

> If you have come to help me, you are wasting your time. But if you have come because your liberation is bound up with mine, then let us work together. (Lilla Watson, Aboriginal elder, educator, and activist)

Overview

Reflecting on the powerful insights in the 10 chapters in *People's Knowledge and Participatory Action Research: Escaping the White-Walled Labyrinth* has been both humbling and inspiring. The contributions have a richness and humanity that academic publications often lack. To even attempt to write a conclusion to such a diverse range of material would, it seems to me, detract from it. However, here I have tried to provide some kind of map, or set of signposts, to allow the reader to navigate the broad territory we define as 'people's knowledge'.

I begin by trying to make sense of the mass of jargon that surrounds inclusive participatory and action research (see Glossary), by looking at three critical traditions of research as a lens through which we can see the different theories and approaches covered in this book. The second section takes a set of practices in which I have repeatedly been involved, widely known as a 'citizens' jury', to argue that the practice of people's knowledge has as much to learn from the artistic and craft traditions as it does from the current obsession, particularly common in social research, with methodological novelty. The third section looks at the ethics of participatory processes, concluding that good ethical practice is much more bound up with our humanity than the institutional codes of ethics that we are often forced to use, or than ethical 'experts' would lead us to believe. The final section was the hardest, but also the most rewarding to write. It is a personal reflection on some of the many mistakes I have made in the 25 years since I started planning my first major initiative aimed at combining social justice, environmental concerns, and the generation of knowledge.

A power map of people's knowledge

> I always say that it is necessary to ask: 'Who's going to know as a result of this research?' 'Whom will this knowledge serve?' 'With whom do I know?' 'Against whom do I know?' 'How do I know?' 'What do I know?' So we discover that these questions clarify this epistemology. (Paulo Freire, educator and philosopher, 1921–97)

For those of us whose expertise comes more from our life experience than from our formal training, having to come to terms with academic jargon is like navigating an obstacle course in a hurricane whilst blindfolded. Technical terms associated with the practices and initiatives described in this book can overcomplicate the argument being made and prevent learning on the part of many readers who might be unfamiliar with specialized language. Already running into hundreds, the number of terms in social and participatory research burgeons with each passing academic trend. Even Paulo Freire, who has provided guidance and inspiration to countless freedom struggles all over the world, often wrote in a style that I, as someone not trained in social science, found to be inaccessible and off-putting. A good example is the final sentence of the quote above. For anyone who has not had an introduction to Western traditions of philosophy, the word 'epistemology' (see Glossary) could discourage them going any further.

Whether you are involved in community-based groups, research institutions, or other types of organization, my aim in this chapter is to help you make sense of the themes of this book. I am aware of my position of white middle-class male privilege. Although I have worked alongside activists pushing for change on a range of issues relating to ecology and social justice, my perspective is biased by the limitations of my own background and, no doubt, by my unconscious prejudices (McIntosh, 1989; Singh, 2016). Whether white middle-class men like me know it or not, we still unfairly dominate the written and broadcast media. This said, I offer the words that follow in the spirit of Lilla Watson's invitation at the beginning of this chapter. My aim is to highlight the perspectives of others writing in this book to as wide an audience as possible.

The Glossary at the end of this book is a brief guide to the words and phrases used in the book from the perspective of power. Even though it uses unnecessary jargon, the quote from Freire that begins this section challenges us to consider the core issue of the relationship between knowledge and power. To this end, Box 11.1 and Table 11.1 explore some of the approaches to research and engagement that authors of this book have encountered.

Three critical traditions of research, business action research, educational action research and participatory action research (PAR), provide a lens through which we can see the different theories and practices covered in this book. A useful description of some of these approaches is provided by Nind (2014). All three traditions have a focus on people's action (Fals Borda and Rahman, 1991), research done inclusively (Nind, 2014), or both. They are meant to work towards altering an outcome of a situation, such that a previously oppressed group can achieve a positive change against more powerful individuals or organizations, or more generally against structural inequality that stems, for example, from racism, class bias, and patriarchy.

To a lesser or greater extent, all three traditions seek to transform power and thus people's relationship to power. Of the three, PAR has perhaps been the most suited to collective struggles by the oppressed to overcome the forces that oppress them. This is hardly surprising, since it explicitly addresses the priorities of oppressed or excluded groups in the formulation of its research questions and strategy. However, understanding the other two traditions is important for those of us interested in PAR. To make progress, we must therefore enter into dialogue with many people who may share our values, but who come from different traditions of participation or action through research. The understanding this yields will allow us to enter a more informed and fruitful dialogue.

The three overlapping traditions of research described in Box 11.1 are displayed in tabular form in Table 11.1, with the addition of black participatory research. To differing degrees at different times and in different contexts, each tradition of action research has been self-critical in its attempts to contribute to struggles for social and ecological justice.

Box 11.1 Three overlapping traditions of research involving 'participation' or 'action'

Business action research. This is the application of action research to business. Social psychologist Kurt Lewin is widely credited with having coined the term 'action research' (Adelman, 1993). From the 1960s, the model of action research he promoted became influential in the study of business and organizational development. Lewin stated that 'only by resolving social conflict, whether it be religious, racial or industrial, can the human condition be improved', and believed action research was the way to do it. However, most of his research was focused on increasing productivity in the workplace, rather than dealing with inequality and social justice. Building on his influential studies, academics have built schools of business action research within business and management departments of universities. In the late 20th century, out of the public eye, this particular type of action research, with its own set of values, aided the growth of power and influence amongst many of the world's largest corporations.

With its main focus being the increase of the market share of a particular corporation, business action research was only rarely used to allow workers to co-design safeguards to protect their rights, at least in the USA and UK. This

(continued)

Box 11.1 Three overlapping traditions of research involving 'participation' or 'action' (*continued*)

continues to be the case, particularly for large corporations who now employ their own in-house action researchers in order to improve their performance. For several decades the links between university management schools and action researchers in corporations dwarfed the links they had with social movements. In 2001 Peter Reason and Hilary Bradbury published the landmark *Handbook of Action Research* and then launched the journal *Action Research*. This has helped build a community that has supported a more varied, and often more challenging, vision for action research in business and beyond.

Educational action research. This draws on the ideas from the business action research tradition. However, educational action researchers recognize that schools and other educational establishments have, or at least should have, different aims to that of a private corporation. Their writing and some practical work draws on diverse accounts of social and political activism, such as the Danish folk school movement, democratic thinkers such as John Dewey and Orlando Fals Borda, feminist educators such as bell hooks, and community organizers such as Myles Horton. Many of those involved in this type of research acknowledge that mainstream educational institutions contain practices (such as the segregation of children based on testing their abilities during their early years) that perpetuate oppression.

Whilst some educational action researchers respond to this challenge by limiting themselves to research that does not risk disrupting the established order, others, such as Wilfred Carr, Stephen Kemmis, and Susan Noffke, have taken a more radical stance. They pioneered 'critical pedagogy' (see Glossary), which is an approach to learning also developed by Paulo Freire, Joe Kincheloe, and bell hooks (Kincheloe, 2008; hooks, 1994). Some educational action researchers work with people outside mainstream educational settings, such as community groups working with people with learning disabilities (Cook, 2012). This type of research is sometimes included under the heading of participatory health research – a field that also touches on patient involvement (see Hale, 2016, and Glossary).

Participatory action research (PAR). PAR exists through many different traditions, amongst peoples of varying cultures and in different languages. Having taken place in purely oral traditions in some parts of the world (e.g. Madhusudhan, 2008; Hale, 2008), it is possible that PAR emerged numerous times amongst communities facing hardship. PAR has grown in popularity amongst social movements and some professional researchers over the past century. A handful of its practitioners have become particularly well known – Orlando Fals Borda, Paulo Freire, Myles Horton, and Anisur Rahman. They were active at the intersection of adult education programmes and social movement building in Latin America (Fals Borda, 1988; Horton and Freire, 1990; Torres, 2014), South Asia (Fals Borda and Rahman, 1991; Rahman, 1993), and the Appalachian Mountains, USA (Horton et al., 1997; Gaventa, 1982).

Freire began his work with the illiterate poor of the city of Pernambuco, Brazil, where he pioneered a radical approach to adult education. He believed that education had two orientations. Firstly, it can function as an instrument to facilitate the integration of generations into the logic of the present system, and bring about conformity to it. Alternatively, education is a 'practice of freedom', the means by which men and women critically analyse this reality, become conscious of oppressions, and discover how to participate in the transformation of their world. It was this insistence that education is a political act that led to the popularization of the term 'critical pedagogy' amongst followers of Freire (Mayo, 1999 and see Glossary).

Over the past century, PAR has emerged as an important contribution to the self-transformation of groups, organizations, and communities. It has left a mark on the field of community development, especially amongst peoples of the Global South (see Glossary) and oppressed groups in the North. Practitioners have developed tools and concepts for doing research with people, including 'barefoot scientists' and grassroots experts-by-experience. They have flourished under the direct guidance of pioneers such as Freire, Horton and, more recently, the City University of New York's Public Science Project, which uses the term Critical PAR to distinguish its self-critical approach from that undertaken by others who use PAR as just another social science research method. Notable self-critical users of PAR include the US civil rights movement; women living with HIV/AIDS globally; the Zapatistas in Chiapas, Mexico; RefugeeYouth in the UK; and the Food Sovereignty Alliance, India. Because it prioritizes communication and critical reflection at the grassroots, rather than via professional academics, PAR is rarely seen in issues of academic journals. However, it has been documented as a series of rich case studies contained in a handful of books (e.g. Horton et al., 1997; Fals Borda and Rahman, 1991; Hale, 2008; Cammarota and Fine, 2008) and practitioner-focused (or 'grey') literature such as the pioneering *Participatory Learning and Action*, a series published by the International Institute for Environment and Development between 1995 and 2013.

However, it is clear to me that the less critical thinking, particularly with regards to power, that takes place within a practice or discipline, the greater the risk that people's democratic right to participate in the creation of knowledge becomes compromised. As Chapters 2, 3 and 6 (Guzman et al., 2016; Mohamed et al., 2016; Pearson et al., 2016) have shown, there is a real danger that the presence of many people's voices becomes an exercise in tokenism, leading to epistemic injustice (see Glossary).

Outside the English-speaking world, the term 'action research' is rarely used. In Germany and some parts of Latin America, it is unpopular with older generations of researchers and some policymakers because of its historic links to Marxism and people's movements. In Germany, the term is still tainted amongst some academics after a mass media campaign against one of its pioneers, the critical psychologist Klaus Holzkamp, in the early 1970s (Teo, 1998). I was once told at an academic conference that if I wanted the Latin American public health researchers or German management researchers to talk to me, I should avoid the term. It made me reflect on how politically charged attempts to challenge the established hierarchy of research can be, particularly when the current trend in neoliberal universities is to marginalize researchers who might threaten traditional power structures within which universities are themselves embedded.

Diverting researchers from reflecting critically on the values and power struggles that underlie the different traditions relating to their area of study is the dazzling array of participatory and action-orientated methodologies on offer. In the sciences, and now increasingly in the social sciences, it is often reported that the use of new methods has led, or will be likely to lead, to a new insight. Researchers can call attention to a new method in the same way as an ingenious new invention. Without implying a criticism of any particular method, some randomly chosen examples include photovoice, citizens' juries, and multicriteria mapping. This thirst for novelty is particularly common amongst those academics with an interest in participatory approaches. It appears that the rate of appearance of new techniques and tools is in inverse proportion to the amount of critical scrutiny to which they are subjected. The celebration of methodological novelty is not just a fashion; it is linked to the way in which academics are trained and rewarded.

Table 11.1 Four traditions of critical action research

Tradition	Features	Practitioners & movements	Publications	Related practices
Participatory action research (PAR)	Research with and by communities who do not have professional research training that emphasizes their participation in the whole process of research and action	Public Science Project (US), RefugeeYouth (UK), women living with HIV/AIDS (global), Zaptatistas (Mexico), Highlander Center (US)	Horton 1998, Fals-Borda & Rahman 1991, Cammarota and Fine 2008 and many non-academic publications ('grey literature')	Critical PAR (CPAR), community-based participatory research (CBPR)
Black participatory research (BPR)	Puts control over the research process in the hands of people of colour	Civil rights movement (US), #BlackLivesMatter, Girijan Deepika (India), Food Sovereignty Alliance (India)	Drame & Irby 2016 describe pioneering work in US government/ state schools. International School of Bottom-up Organising (Latin America)	Shares values of much PAR and feminist action research
Educational action research (EAR)	Education-related research carried out inclusively with the intention of achieving greater social justice	bell hooks (US), Stephen Kemmis (Australia), Susan Noffke (US), Melanie Nind (UK)	*Educational Action Research* (journal)	Patient involvement, participatory health research
Business action research (BAR)	Research and organizational learning that is undertaken within the capitalist economic system with the intention of improving ethical outcomes	Peter Reason (UK), Hilary Bradbury (US), Yoland Wadsworth (Australia)	*Action Research* (journal)	Management organizational development, feminist action research

More than ever, most of our research takes place in the context of the neoliberal (see Glossary) system of capitalism. Sociologist Steve Fuller has linked the drive for ever faster production of novelty in research to the concept of 'fast capitalism'. Fast capitalism is the tendency of capitalist systems to extract surplus value with as little investment as possible for the greatest possible return, whilst adding as little to the real economy as possible, often by means of financial speculation and the manufacturing of goods with 'planned obsolescence' (Agger, 2004). The classic example of fast capitalism is the iPhone, where each new model brings with it a series of software upgrades that soon make previous models obsolete. This is the necessary consequence of neoliberal systems of capitalism, made even faster by pervasive digital technologies.

With universities increasingly resembling neoliberal corporations, Fuller coined the term 'fast science' to describe how scientists (and increasingly other researchers) are encouraged to generate results that are just different enough from previous results to ensure publication. 'Fast science' resembles fast food, says Fuller, as it endeavours to 'maximize waste by ever quickening cycles of resource use and disposal' (Fuller and Collier, 2003).

In academic research into participation, the application of a new technique is seen as more interesting than mere repetition. The context-dependent craft skills (known as 'bricolage' – see Glossary) are thus discriminated against in the publication process. This is in stark contrast to the arts, where an artist's ability is traditionally measured not in terms of invention, but in their capacity to combine traditional motifs in new and challenging ways (Hallam and Ingold, 2007). To worldwide acclaim, the sculptor Antony Gormley has produced many hundreds of unique artworks by repeatedly reproducing his own form in cast iron, metal poles, and, occasionally, ice.

Eight citizens' juries

As with many humanistic practices, it is often said of participatory research that it is 'more of an art than a science'. It is time to take this aphorism seriously and escape from social research's fetish for the novel at the expense of understanding context. I propose that we attempt to learn from some occasions in which I have undertaken particular processes of participatory action research, as someone who works with the materials they've got: a 'bricoleur' (see Glossary; Wakeford and Pimbert, 2013).

The citizens' jury is an approach to participation that has been repeated hundreds of times (Coote and Lenaghan, 1997; Jefferson Center, 2004; Kashefi and Keene, 2008; Kuruganti et al., 2008; Wakeford, 2012; Wakeford et al., 2015). Of the times I have been involved in organizing, supporting, and studying these processes over 17 years, I have chosen eight case studies to illustrate the importance of context.

With each repetition of this particular approach to participation, I reflected and learned. The best participatory research came not from me aiming to create a perfect methodology for all participatory research, but by improvising based on my past experience in response to each unique context. Here I describe this process of bricolage in the context of eight citizens' juries that took place over a period of 10 years from 1998 to 2008.

Jury 1

In 1998, shortly after finishing a PhD in the natural sciences, I began a formal role as a participatory worker for a small UK-based non-governmental organization called Genetics Forum. I had never undertaken a citizens' jury, or any other piece of participatory research before. Working from a handbook (Coote and Lenaghan, 1997) and with a technique contributed by my science policy researcher colleagues (Stirling and Mayer, 1999), I improvised the design and delivery of the process. My volunteer participants were 15 men and women from all walks of life. Combining ideas gleaned from my brief research with some on-the-spot improvisation, I oversaw a citizens' jury process that became known as 'Citizen Foresight'.

Following the general guidelines in Coote and Lenaghan's handbook, my team established an oversight panel as a way of improving the quality of the process and as a safeguard against accusations of bias. Having interrogated eight specialist commentators with diverse perspectives on the complex set of scientific, economic, and political issues under discussion, the participants reached a set of informed conclusions.

In addition to organizing and chairing proceedings, my job was to use these outputs for media work. As the jury's recommendations challenged established wisdom, I put forward volunteer participants to defend the process in public. My final task, as a full-time academic researcher, was to write a report on the process (Wakeford, 1999), discuss the work at conferences, and join academic colleagues in ongoing analyses of participatory processes (Irwin, 2001; Wakeford, 2002).

The learning that most stood out for me was:

- Some participants – particularly one from a manual work background – said almost nothing, at least when I was in the room.
- Some of the scientific 'experts' appeared to mislead the participants on matters of fact. On a couple of occasions they were corrected on important matters of fact by the participants.
- Making a video archive of proceedings was vital. One of the members of the oversight panel wrote to me suggesting that my participatory work might have biased the process against a particular technology of which he was an advocate. I sent him a video of all the proceedings. Having watched them, he was satisfied that there was no obvious bias.
- I failed to involve the jury in planning the publicity that followed the report. The drive to maximize publicity took precedent over a PAR approach of letting the group decide what strategy to use and who should be involved.
- I did not give the participants sufficient support to develop their capacity as participatory researchers. They did not have the opportunity to reflect together on the participatory research of which they were part. To that extent I did them what Miranda Fricker (2007) would call a heuristic injustice (see Glossary) – I denied them sufficient opportunity to learn about the process in which they were involved.

Jury 2

In 1999, I moved to India, where I undertook a second citizens' jury, this time for a large international development charity. I was working with an Indian civil servant who had been seconded to the charity. I spent six months living in South India undertaking background research in rural areas and meeting people who would be participants in the jury, either as 'jurors' or as experts. My limited experience of the country was a major barrier to understanding the context – both social and cultural – in which the jury would take place. I had to balance this with an implicit expectation from the charity's campaigns department, which was the sole funder of the process, that the jury should take place within a few months of my arrival in the country. I failed to find anyone with experience of participation who spoke the local language. I felt I had no choice but to leave the facilitation of the process to a civil servant who at least had received some minimal training in theoretical aspects of participatory research. His membership of a high caste and his inability to speak in rural dialects meant that he could not be fully understood by, nor could he fully understand, the participants. The same went for many of those specialist commentators who appeared before the citizens' jury process.

By the end of the process it was clear that we had not developed a capability amongst the jurors to allow them to come up with their own conclusions. The on-the-spot judgement my Indian colleague and I made was that all they could be asked to do was vote. In the chaos of multiple languages and caste hierarchies the wrong question was put to them and hence they undertook a meaningless vote. By the time the corrected question had been put to them and a vote had taken place, I was beginning to have serious reservations about the extent to which the jury could be called participatory research. Apart from the jury being 'heard' via a superficial vote, the jury failed in that it did not redress either heuristic or testimonial injustice (see Glossary).

Myself and my funder gained some deeper reflections during the process through the presence of a participatory researcher with long experience of working in rural India. They suggested ways of improving the process in future. The learning my colleagues and I took from this included the following suggestions for future jury processes:

- Try to resist pressure to undertake participatory research without being sure you have sufficiently participatory workers, along with a contingency plan.
- Develop safeguards against a situation where one funder becomes a dominant force, such that the participatory research becomes more of a performance than a legitimate intellectual and self-critical exercise.
- Have critical friends on hand to ensure that you can learn from your mistakes. As a participatory worker you are not in a good position to do that yourself.

Jury 3

Still in India, the participatory researcher who helped me learn lessons from Jury 2 was approached by local civil society organizations (CSOs) who were concerned about a World Bank and UK Government investment plan. Together with the CSOs, I spent a year with him organizing a large-scale citizens' jury that allowed the jurors both to learn about the projects planned for their region, and to become sufficiently well informed that they could envision their own development plan called Vision 2020 (Pimbert and Wakeford, 2003). Two participatory workers who spoke the same dialect as the jurors helped them to develop their conclusions. Overseen by a retired Chief of the Supreme Court, we built in safeguards against the participants being intimidated by the presence of powerful agencies, elite scientists, and the media. The jury were able to write their own conclusions.

The report of the process had a major impact regionally, nationally, and internationally. The UK Government's response was to claim that the process was biased (Wakeford and Pimbert, 2004; Kuruganti et al., 2008; Wakeford and Pimbert, 2013). Under pressure from the UK Government, my research institute and the UK-based CSO where my co-author was based withdrew the report, without any consultation with the Indian organizations. It was later reinstated. However, the reputations of both the organizations that had first published and then undermined the report were damaged: they lost credibility amongst social movements for their lack of independence from government. In undertaking this jury we learned that:

- This jury was a far better fit to the social and political context than Jury 2. It is worth raising sufficient funds for a process in which considerable time can be spent building up grassroots capacity, and in which few corners are cut in order to save money.
- Whatever the subject of the participatory research – particularly if it is controversial – having the research overseen by an oversight body containing all shades of opinion is essential.
- Even if you are attempting the best participatory work possible, don't assume your research institute will back you if the conclusions threaten their interests.

Jury 4

This time in Brazil, I provided advice to the same international development charity that had funded Jury 2 on designing a citizens' jury on an issue of public policy importance. Within minutes of the jury beginning it became clear that the participatory workers had a very different approach to a citizens' jury to the one I had envisaged. Deliberate or not, this was pseudo-participation as spectacle. There was no heuristic justice being achieved. There was only testimonial justice, to the extent that the city's governing party was taking a stand against a multinational chemical company. Using as participatory an approach as I could, I conducted a study of the process, which was presented back to the charity. The main lesson I took from this experience was that the appearance of research being participatory can sometimes be deceptive, particularly in cultural and political contexts with which the researcher is unfamiliar. Rather than promoting greater understanding of an issue, or allowing the shared control of research with people who have previously been excluded, such processes can be used as a means of providing media headlines that merely support a pre-existing point of view held by the organization that funds the jury.

Jury 5

I advised on helping set up a citizens' jury in Zimbabwe, using funding from one of the world's largest charitable foundations based in New York. Local partner organizations were also involved. The process went smoothly. However, a major problem emerged in that the funder wanted the jury process to discuss the impact of a new technology, whereas the communities from which the jurors were drawn were in a situation of near famine due to the economic position of Zimbabwe at that time. However much the local participatory workers tried, they struggled to get hungry, frightened people to focus on something as abstract as a new technology, despite it being an issue considered by distant policymakers as of major importance for their futures (Coupe et al., 2005). I felt implicated in a process whereby social researchers were using their power to determine the agenda for a participatory process, which appeared unethical in the circumstances. To be justified, I think there has to be a much more urgent policy objective than the one provided by the directors of the research.

Jury 6

Until now, the subject focus of each of the citizens' juries in which I had been a participatory worker had been more or less determined by the jury's funders. In a northern UK city, we tried to allow those experiencing oppression to set the topic for the jury. A small team of workers assembled a range of older people (which in the UK means over 50 years old) living on average or below-average incomes. Most were involved with social movements of one sort or another. We organized a series of meetings to allow around 20 people to analyse the most important issues that affected them. After considering issues such as transport, pensions, ageism, and building design, they decided to focus on the health system – specifically the way in which it deals with older people who have falls. They oversaw the way in which the issue was framed for the jury, the invitation of potential jurors, and my and my colleagues' conduct of the participatory work.

We used the term 'do-it-yourself' citizens' jury, and set up an oversight body made up of people with knowledge of, or decision-making power over, the issues covered by the jury. The jury came to one conclusion that the head of the local health authority found unhelpful. Despite all our groundwork, the jury's conclusions were thus not welcomed by the main organization they were intended to influence – the local health authority. The lessons our team of participatory workers learned included:

- A process of participatory research, such as a DIY citizens' jury, is closer to the ideals of PAR in that it allows the focus of the study to be co-determined by formally trained researchers and people whose expertise comes from their life experience.
- Allowing people from marginalized backgrounds to decide the issue to be discussed by the jury gave the whole process greater democratic legitimacy and transparency.

- Groups with interests that they believe to be threatened by the participatory research process will do their best to avoid being exposed to public scrutiny, by attempting to ensure that the process does not get media coverage.

Jury 7

The charity that funded Jury 6 shared my concern about the rise of far-right political groups in the UK, particularly in parts of the north of England. In these areas of economic deprivation, there were increasing numbers of racist attacks – both verbal and physical – on ethnic minority communities. The charity worked with us to design a participatory research programme using a DIY citizens' jury (see Jury 6). We and the charity's trustees believed that this jury could find issues that were not being addressed by the council, and bring different communities together in finding ways of moving forward together. The jury chose two issues: firstly, the increased use of illegal drugs and its link to property crime; secondly, the increasing city centre disorder due to excess alcohol consumption.

The jurors built up a sophisticated critique of the way in which government policy had worsened the problems of alcohol and illegal drugs in the local community. Their analysis was shared with elected policymakers in a video, made by an activist film-maker. Our desired side-effect of the participatory research, that intercultural dialogue took place, was also achieved. Several of the white English jury members were able to get to know people of Indian and Pakistani ethnocultural heritage for the first time. It provided some jury members with their first experience of intercultural dialogue and led to some of those from predominantly white English cultural backgrounds to embrace non-European cultures and languages of which they had previously been suspicious. The same process appeared to take place amongst some of the people of colour on the jury.

The charity agreed to help extend the research, both amongst additional members of the local community and in a second DIY jury in a town experiencing similar problems in a neighbouring district. However, no funding was available to help extend and deepen this participatory work beyond short-term work in these two districts. In the 2015 UK general election, a political party seen by many as embodying racism gained 3 million votes across England, coming second in 120 constituencies – many of them in northern England. I believe that if the process we began in this area had been scaled up sufficiently across the UK, such a rise in racist attitudes amongst UK voters could have been checked.

Amongst the lessons we learned from this process were:

- PAR can be a powerful way to build community in racially divided cities.
- A small minority of the participants said little or nothing during the process. It was hard to tell whether this silence was due to people's experience of their voices not counting for anything in other forums, a lack of confidence, or the fact that they were there out of desperation for the small payment that was given to all participants.
- In one of the cities, two senior police officers offered an analysis of why some Asian members of the community had a higher rate of arrest that

was, by any interpretation, based on racist assumptions. Since their comments were stated in public and recorded on video, we should have done more to challenge this behaviour at the time or subsequently.

Jury 8

We adapted the citizens' jury approach used in Jury 7 to work on two issues in parallel – one raised by local people from marginalized social backgrounds, the other dictated by the UK Government's science department. We called the process a 'community x-change' and conducted a series of workshops over two weekends involving people from a region in eastern England. Sensing that formal techniques of participatory research would fail to engage some of the more vulnerable people involved in the workshops, one of us used his background in youth work to develop a participatory theatre performance with them. This was performed at the end of the first day and appeared to provide inspiration for all those from the local community who had become involved. The science-based organization we were working with was extremely nervous about moving away from a model of participation based on science education. We used a participatory research approach to work with them to reflect on the process, so that we could deepen our understanding of what had taken place. Amongst the conclusions of this reflection was that we should:

- employ someone with a long-term relationship with members of the local community as a co-convenor of future processes
- engage in a longer-term process to build up links between those living in the local community who were scientists – who were largely middle class – and the marginalized members of the local community who had expertise, gained through life experience, which had not been taken seriously previously
- open up discussions about the subtle institutional racism that exists in organizations.

Reflections on eight citizens' juries

These juries took place over eight years in the chronological order in which they are presented here. It is nine years since the events described in Jury 8. I am at the beginning of a process of reflecting on the experience with others (e.g. Kashefi and Mort, 2004; Singh, 2008). I am drawn to Elham Kashefi's use of grounded theory for this purpose. This operates almost in a reverse fashion from social science as most commonly practised (see 'scientism' in Glossary), as it often begins with the collection of qualitative data, rather than a theory or hypothesis. As researchers review the data collected, repeated themes, concepts, or elements become apparent.

Together with colleagues, I have explored the repeated themes that have emerged elsewhere (Wakeford et al., 2015). In summary, I have strengthened my and other participatory workers' understanding of our practice through a process of bricolage, and then reflection, on each individual jury.

Reflecting on 17 years as a participatory researcher, I have concluded that participation is not necessarily best seen as a method of research. Instead, drawing on the work of organizations such as RefugeeYouth (2009) and individuals such as Brydon-Miller (Brydon-Miller and Stoecker, 2013), Pimbert (Borrini-Feyerabend et al., 2013; Pimbert et al., 2010), Freire, Horton and Fals Borla (Horton et al., 1997; Fals Borla and Rahman, 1991), I think it is best viewed as set of politically engaged practices that redefines what constitutes research. To paraphrase feminist action researcher Patricia Maguire, I am not a social scientist interested in a more participatory approach to research, but a worker and activist exploring alternative approaches to research as one tool in the struggle for a more just, loving world (cited in Reason and Bradbury, 2001: 1).

There are of course many methodologies that can be useful for participatory research. Like tools in a toolbox, their various features should be understood. We need to understand what type of structure we are building (or repairing), why, and with whom. Similarly, the methods used in participatory work need to be understood in the overall social, cultural, and political context in which they are being used. Having a big toolkit of methods does not guarantee any one of them will be sufficient on its own. The citizens' jury example demonstrates that the best way of learning about such approaches is to do so in the context in which they are applied. The effective use of any approach relies more on craft skills acquired over time than any particular methodology.

Ethical principles and practice

Is it helpful to attempt to formulate a set of principles for good participatory work? Until recently, claims that guidelines and codes of practice are the best way of improving outcomes in participatory work have gone largely unchallenged. From early in my experience of participatory research I have seen such codes apparently ignored. Some instances became well documented by researchers (e.g. Wallace, 2001; Davies et al., 2006). In the UK it took a group of investigative journalists and environmental activists to highlight how widespread the problem had become. Following a complaint from a participant, they exposed how a prominent member of the Market Research Association – the UK industry's trade and certification body – had flouted its guidelines on ethical research (Wakeford and Singh, 2008: 51).

Anthropologists criticize ethical codes for acting as a kind of 'constitution' for professional academics (Meskell and Pels, 2005). Studies of participatory research with people living with HIV/AIDS suggest that such codes encourage researchers into becoming *de facto* adjudicators and so, on the basis of this ethical constitution and supposed mastery of ethical information language, allow them to assume a position of superiority in work with non-academics (Vazquez and Hale, 2011). Like many institutionalized procedures, they risk mainly protecting the professionals and their institutions, rather than those people with less power. In attempting a transcendent set of guidelines, they also depoliticize the issues they raise (Mouffe, 2013).

Codes can too frequently be a tick-box proceduralism of the kind that has been condemned by inquiries into failed health systems, such as in the UK's mid-Staffordshire hospital scandal. It would be possible for a team of participatory workers to follow the letter of all the principles and guidelines (such as the Principles and Guidelines of the International Collaboration for Participatory Health 2013) and for the work to take place against a background level of structural violence such that there is a risk people are left worse off. I suggest that a preferable alternative might be to explore what has been called non-procedural, or discourse, ethics, through dialogue with those groups who could be said to use such approaches. Such groups might include the Public Science Project (Cammarota and Fine, 2008; Stoudt et al., 2015; Torres, 2014; RefugeeYouth, 2009; see also Guzman et al., 2016; Mohamed et al., 2016; Pearson et al., 2016).

It is common sense that 'caring about people' is an essential prerequisite of participatory research. Lynn Froggett's work traces the origin of a human being's capacity to care 'not in some optimum form of socialization, but in the existing emotional repertoires of most people who have experienced good-enough parenting'. In other words, caring is not a set of skills or beliefs that need to be learned, but something inherent in all human beings, unless we have been deeply psychologically damaged (Froggett, 2002: 150). Should adults who have not been damaged in such a way, let alone participatory researchers, really need a code to tell us how to be human?

The competence of participatory research processes can be fatally undermined by a fundamental weakness in design: the sponsorship of the participatory research by a single powerful interest group. It is described in Jury 4 and was also dramatically highlighted by the Francis Inquiry into the mid-Staffordshire scandal. Here, patient involvement (a form of participatory research) was co-opted in to serve competing organizational objectives within a large bureaucracy. Though little documented to date, many will be aware of research conducted by academics that has seen participatory work pulled towards serving the interests of, or questions framed by, the university department and its funders. Sometimes these may be at odds with the interests of the communities they claim to serve.

As an alternative to the much criticized ethical checklists based on established principles of research conduct, Alissa Cordner and colleagues have proposed a framework of 'reflexive research ethics' that takes into account the 'dynamic relationships between multiple parties or the constant uncertainty faced by researchers as they navigate new ethical terrain or face questions unaddressed by existing standards' (Cordner et al., 2012: 162). They also challenge the claim that research must be disinterested in order to be done with integrity. Instead they suggest that genuine research integrity is about 'engaging with ethics as fluid, dynamic and value-laden guideposts that must be constantly and self-consciously reflected upon' (Cordner et al., 2012: 171).

Cordner suggests that good research with community partners involves an acknowledgement that the identification of the rights to which individuals and communities are entitled, and the choice of which practices should be employed, are contested issues, and thus demand constant reflexivity (see Glossary) on the part of researchers.

People's Knowledge and Participatory Action Research and the People's Knowledge Editorial Collective are helping to open up spaces where participatory workers and participants can tell stories about their experiences in order to allow learning to take place beyond.

Like Cordner, I believe that research must be seen as credible in order to contribute to the legitimacy and successes of community-based collaborators. This requires researchers to not only actively use, but also move beyond, forms of ethical conduct, such as individual informed consent, that are codified in institutional protocols. These institutional requirements may be important for research and may (or may not) provide necessary safeguards for research participants. However, when studying organizations, communities, and groups, institutional ethical checklists often do not go far enough. Instead, seeing ethical obligations as reflexive and relational acknowledges the inviolable importance of informed consent, whilst also recognizing that salient ethical concerns emerge during the course of participatory research that are unavoidably contextual, relational, culturally specific, and dependent on the worldviews of those involved.

Approaches that value people's knowledge do not only reject the scientism described in 'The original citizen scientists' (People's Knowledge Editorial Collective, 2016); they also open up the possibility of a more open-minded process of inquiry. As all the chapters of this book demonstrate, we are just at the beginning of seeing what such an approach might achieve. By building a stronger community in solidarity with groups experiencing injustice all over the world, we might yet escape the white-walled labyrinth.

A letter to myself, the young scientist

> Lord, give me the confidence of a mediocre white man. (Tweet by Sarah Hagi, writer, 21 January 2015)[1]

Dear younger self,

You made your family very proud when, aged 21, you organized a conference called 'Science for the Earth'. It was about saving the world. The speakers were not just made up of scientists, such as Stephen Hawking and Lynn Margulis and those they worked with, but also sociologists. There were also activists, such as Sue Mayer from Greenpeace, and many students from an elite university.

You were inspired by those in the 1960s and '70s who had called for a 'science for the people'. Organizations such as Scientists Against Nuclear Arms and the Union of Concerned Scientists foresaw scientists using their puzzle-solving abilities for peace and ecological sustainability, rather than the military-industrial complex. But you had a big blind spot – privilege. Although brought up by a feminist mother and an actively pro-feminist father, you did not really understand the experience of gender oppression. You listened to the US rappers Public Enemy and felt you understood the politics of civil rights, but had only the faintest inkling of the lived experience of racism or colonialism. It took you a long time to learn that you can't truly understand your own white male (and for that matter able-bodied, middle-class, and English-speaking) privilege until you engage with those who have few or no markers of privilege.

Twenty-five years later, I wish you'd made more of an effort, young man! The book you produced as a result of the conference had a chapter by an author of colour questioning the colonialism of much 'modern' science (Alvares, 1995). Yet, it took you another 14 years to spend any time in a former European colony, and another five years after that to work on an anti-racism initiative with people of colour from your own country (see Jury 7). It was only when you experienced your exercise of white male privilege being challenged by people you trusted as colleagues (e.g. see Guzman et al., 2016; Pearson et al., 2016) that you learned its true meaning.

It's too easy for you and I, and people like us, to continue to exercise our privilege (sometimes consciously, but mainly unconsciously) in research settings, such as neoliberal universities, where productivity (or 'fast science') is valued over critical thinking.

So, young reader, don't rely on universities or other research institutions to build your critical faculties! Instead, build relationships with people and movements who are striving to overcome oppression by supporting their efforts. Get out of the lab and the ivory tower, put your career on hold if necessary, and join the struggle. This doesn't mean ditching your critical faculties. On the contrary, it is likely to hone them by what you learn from those who may have had less formal education than yourself.

Make good the mistakes of your youth and march with women campaigning for safer streets; stand alongside refugees subject to inhuman treatment from the authorities; join Dalits in India blockading universities to protest against their systematic exclusion from higher education. You will discover things about yourself that will make you a more useful human being and a better researcher.

Yours sincerely,
Tom

Acknowledgements

Although Tom Wakeford has compiled this chapter, it is the product of dialogue between himself and others in the People's Knowledge Editorial Collective and many others (see Acknowledgements). He would particularly like to thank Colin Anderson, Fiona Hale and Jasber Singh for their critical feedback on earlier drafts.

Note

1. Thanks to Zoe Young for passing on this tweet, which has since become widely shared on social media

References

Adelman, C. (1993) 'Kurt Lewin and the origins of action research', *Educational Action Research* 1: 7–24, <http://dx.doi.org/10.1080/0965079930010102>.

Agger, B. (2004) *Speeding Up Fast Capitalism: Cultures, Jobs, Families, Schools, Bodies*, Routledge, London and New York, NY.

Alvares, C. (1995) 'Does the real world need "modern" science?', in T. Wakeford and M. Walters (eds), *Science for the Earth: Can Science Make the World a Better Place?* Wiley, New York, NY.

Borrini-Feyerabend, G., Farvar, M.T., Renard, Y., Pimbert, M.P. and Kothari, A. (2013) *Sharing Power: A Global Guide to Collaborative Management of Natural Resources*, Routledge, Abingdon.

Brydon-Miller, M. and Stoecker, R. (2013) 'Community covenantal ethics: case studies in community-based research', in S. Goff (ed.), *From Theory to Practice; Context in Praxis: Selected Papers from the 8th Action Learning Action Research World Congress*, pp. 229–30, World Congress on Action Learning, Melbourne, <www.cultureshift.com.au/files/file/Goff_editor's%20preface.pdf> [accessed 11 August 2016].

Cammarota, J. and Fine, M. (eds) (2008) *Revolutionizing Education: Youth Participatory Action Research in Motion*, Routledge, New York, NY.

Cook, T. (2012) 'Where participatory approaches meet pragmatism in funded (health) research: the challenge of finding meaningful spaces', *Forum Qualitative Sozialforschung / Forum: Qualitative Social Research* 13(1) <www.qualitative-research.net/index.php/fqs/article/view/1783/3304> [accessed 11 August 2016].

Coote, A. and Lenaghan, J. (1997) *Citizens' Juries: Theory into Practice*, Institute for Public Policy Research, London.

Cordner, A., Ciplet, D., Brown, P. and Morello-Frosch, R. (2012) 'Reflexive research ethics for environmental health and justice: academics and movement building', *Social Movement Studies* 11: 161–76.

Coupe, S., Hellin, J., Masendeke, A. and Rusike, E.A. (2005) *Farmers' Jury: The Future of Smallholder Farming in Zimbabwe*, Practical Action Publishing, Rugby.

Davies, C., Wetherell, M.S. and Barnett, E. (2006) *Citizens at the Centre: Deliberative Participation in Healthcare Decisions*, The Policy Press, Bristol.

Etmanski C., Hall, B. and Dawson T. (eds) (2014) *Learning and Teaching Community-Based Research: Linking Pedagogy to Practice*, University of Toronto Press, Toronto.

Fals Borda, O (1988) *Knowledge and People's Power: Lessons with Peasants in Nicaragua, Mexico and Columbia*, Indian Social Institute, New Delhi.

Fals Borda, O. and Rahman, A. (1991) *Action and Knowledge: Breaking the Monopoly with Participatory Action Research*, Apex Press, New York; Intermediate Technology Publications, London. Available from: <http://bookzz.org/book/825112/3bbf43> [accessed 11 August 2016].

Fricker, M (2007) *Epistemic Injustice: Power and the Ethics of Knowing*, Oxford University Press, Oxford.

Froggett, L. (2002) *Love, Hate and Welfare: Psychosocial Approaches to Policy and Practice*, The Policy Press, Bristol.

Fuller, S. and Collier, J.H. (2003) *Philosophy, Rhetoric, and the End of Knowledge: A New Beginning for Science and Technology Studies*, Routledge, London and New York, NY.

Gaventa, J. (1982) *Power and Powerlessness: Quiescence and Rebellion in an Appalachian Valley*, University of Illinois Press, Champaign, IL. Available from: <http://bookzz.org/book/906569/27ca26> [accessed 11 August 2016].

Guzman, M., Kadima, C., Lovell, G., Mohamed, A.A., Norton, R., Rivas, F. and Thiam, A. (2016) 'Making connections in the "white-walled labyrinth"', in People's Knowledge Editorial Collective (eds), *People's Knowledge and Participatory Action Research: Escaping the White-Walled Labyrinth*, pp. 23–32, Practical Action Publishing, Rugby <http://dx.doi.org/10.3362/9781780449395.003>.

Hale, C.R. (2008) *Engaging Contradictions: Theory, Politics, and Methods of Activist Scholarship*, University of California Press, Oakland, CA. Available from: <http://bookzz.org/book/848176/a1981a> [accessed 11 August 2016].

Hale, T. (2016) 'LIVErNORTH: combining individual and collective patient knowledge', in People's Knowledge Editorial Collective (eds), *People's Knowledge and Participatory Action Research: Escaping the White-Walled Labyrinth*, pp. 93–102, Practical Action Publishing, Rugby <http://dx.doi.org/10.3362/9781780449395.010>.

Hallam, E. and Ingold, T. (2007) *Creativity and Cultural Improvisation*, Berg, Oxford.

hooks, b. (1994) *Teaching to Transgress: Education as the Practice of Freedom*, Routledge, London and New York, NY.

Horton, M. and Freire, P. (1990) *We Make the Road by Walking: Conversations on Education and Social Change*, Temple University Press, Philadelphia, PA.

Horton, M. with Kohl, J. and Kohl, H. (1997) *The Long Haul: An Autobiography*, Doubleday, New York, NY. Available from: <http://bookzz.org/book/2552014/13b385> [accessed 11 August 2016].

International Collaboration for Participatory Health Research (ICPHR) (2013) *Participatory Health Research: A Guide to Ethical Principles and Practice Principles and Guidelines*, ICPHR, Berlin. Available from: <http://www.icphr.org/uploads/2/0/3/9/20399575/ichpr_position_paper_2_ethics_-_version_october_2013.pdf> [accessed 11 August 2016].

International Institute for Environment and Development (IIED) (1995–2013) *Participatory Learning and Action*, Journal series [online archive], IIED <http://www.iied.org/participatory-learning-action> [accessed 10 August 2016].

Irwin, A. (2001) 'Constructing the scientific citizen: science and democracy in the biosciences', *Public Understanding of Science*, 10: 1–18.

Jefferson Center (2004) *Citizens' Jury® Handbook*, Jefferson Center, Saint Paul, MN. Available from: <www.epfound.ge/files/citizens_jury_handbook.pdf> [accessed 11 August 2016].

Kashefi, E. and Mort, M. (2004) 'Grounded citizens' juries: a tool for health activism?', *Health Expectations* 7: 290–302.

Kashefi, E. and Keene, C. (2008) 'Citizens' juries in Burnley, UK: from deliberation to intervention', *Participatory Learning and Action* 58: 33–8, <http://pubs.iied.org/G02855.html> [accessed 11 August 2016].

Kincheloe, J.L. (2008) *Knowledge and Critical Pedagogy*, Springer, Dordrecht. Available from: <http://bookzz.org/book/877138/406b55> [accessed 11 August 2016].

Kuruganti, K., Pimbert, M. and Wakeford, T. (2008) 'The people's vision: UK and Indian reflections on Prajateerpu', *Participatory Learning and Action* 58: 11–17, <http://pubs.iied.org/G02529.html> [accessed 11 August 2016].

Madhusudhan (2008) 'Girijana Deepika: challenges for a people's organization in Andhra Pradesh, India', *Participatory Learning and Action* 58: 97–103, <http://pubs.iied.org/G02867.html> [accessed 11 August 2016].

Mayo, P. (1999) *Gramsci, Freire and Adult Education: Possibilities for Transformative Action*, Palgrave Macmillan, London and New York, NY.

McIntosh, P (1989) 'White privilege: unpacking the invisible knapsack', Wellesley College Center for Research on Women, Wellesley, MA. Available from: <https://www.deanza.edu/faculty/lewisjulie/White%20Priviledge%20Unpacking%20the%20Invisible%20Knapsack.pdf> [accessed 19 September 2016].

Meskell, L. and Pels, P. (eds) (2005) *Embedding Ethics: Shifting Boundaries of the Anthropological Profession*, Berg, New York. https://www.deanza.edu/faculty/lewisjulie/White%20Priviledge%20Unpacking%20the%20Invisible%20Knapsack.pdf

Mohamed, A.A., Istwani, A., Villate, B., Ohberg, E., Galante, E., Mohamed, F., Ahmed, I., Smith, H.M., Pearson, L., Guzman, M., Istwani, S., Sakar, S., Hunter-Darch, S. and Miah, T. (2016) 'Examining our differences', in People's Knowledge Editorial Collective (eds), *People's Knowledge and Participatory Action Research: Escaping the White-Walled Labyrinth*, pp. 33–44, Practical Action Publishing, Rugby <http://dx.doi.org/10.3362/9781780449395.004>.

Mouffe, C. (2013) *Agonistics: Thinking the World Politically*, Verso Books, London and Brooklyn, NY.

Nind, M. (2014) *What is Inclusive Research?* Bloomsbury, London.

Pearson, L., Sanchez Rodriguez, J. and Mohamed, A.A. (2016) 'A puzzling search for authenticity within academia, in People's Knowledge Editorial Collective (eds), *People's Knowledge and Participatory Action Research: Escaping the White-Walled Labyrinth*, pp. 63–72, Practical Action Publishing, Rugby <http://dx.doi.org/10.3362/9781780449395.007>.

People's Knowledge Editorial Collective (2016) 'The original citizen scientists', in People's Knowledge Editorial Collective (eds), *People's Knowledge and Participatory Action Research: Escaping the White-Walled Labyrinth*, pp. 103–112, Practical Action Publishing, Rugby, <http://dx.doi.org/10.3362/9781780449395.011 >.

Pimbert, M. and Wakeford, T. (2003) 'Prajateerpu, power and knowledge: the politics of participatory action research in development. Part I: Context, process and safeguards', *Action Research* 1: 184–207.

Pimbert, M.P., Barry, B., Berson, A. and Tran-Thanh, K. (2010) *Democratising Agricultural Research for Food Sovereignty in West Africa*, Reclaiming Diversity and Citizenship series, IIED, London. Available from: <http://pubs.iied. org/14603IIED.html> [accessed 11 August 2016].

Rahman, M.A. (1993) *People's Self-Development: Perspectives on Participatory Action Research. A Journey Through Experience*, Zed Books, Vancouver.

Reason, P. and Bradbury, H. (2001) *Handbook of Action Research: Participative Inquiry and Practice*, Sage Publications, London. Available from: <http:// bookzz.org/book/1102577/186764> [accessed 11 August 2016].

RefugeeYouth (2009) *Becoming a Londoner: Our Creative Campaign*, RefugeeYouth, London.

Singh, J. (2008) 'The UK Nanojury as 'upstream' public engagement', *Participatory Learning and Action* 58: 27–32, <http://pubs.iied.org/G02854.html> [accessed 11 August 2016].

Singh, J. (2016) 'Cultivating an anti-racist position in post-race society', in People's Knowledge Editorial Collective (eds), *People's Knowledge and Participatory Action Research: Escaping the White-Walled Labyrinth*, pp. 45–52, Practical Action Publishing, Rugby <http://dx.doi. org/10.3362/9781780449395.005>.

Stirling, A. and Mayer, S. (1999) *Rethinking Risk: A Pilot Multi-Criteria Mapping of a Genetically Modified Crop in Agricultural Systems in the UK*, Science Policy Research Unit, University of Sussex, Brighton.

Stoudt, B.G., Torre, M.E., Bartley, P., Bracy, F., Caldwell, H., Downs, A., Greene, C., Haldipur, J., Hassan, P., Manoff, E., Sheppard, N. and Yates, J. (2015) 'Participatory action research and policy change', in C. Durose and L. Richardson (eds), *Designing Public Policy for Co-Production: Theory, Practice and Change*, The Policy Press, Brighton.

Teo, T. (1998) 'Klaus Holzkamp and the rise and decline of German critical psychology', *History of Psychology* 1: 235.

Torres, C.A. (2014) *First Freire: Early Writings in Social Justice Education*, Teachers' College Press, New York, NY and London.

Vazquez, M.J. and Hale, F. (2011) 'Ethical considerations for an integral response to human rights, HIV and violence against women in Central America' [online], Inter-American Commission of Women of the Organization of American States, <www.oas.org/en/cim/docs/VIH-VAW-ConsideracionesEticas-EN.pdf> [accessed 11 August 2016].

Wakeford, T. (1999) *Citizen Foresight: A Tool to Enhance Democratic Policy Making. 1: The Future of Food and Agriculture*, Genetics Forum and University of East London, London.

Wakeford, T. (2002) 'Citizens' juries: a radical alternative for social research', *Social Research Update* 37: 1–5.

Wakeford, T. (2012) *Teach Yourself Citizens' Juries*, 2nd edn, Edinburgh University, Edinburgh. Available from: <www.researchgate.net/publication/275218861_Teach_Yourself_Citizens_Juries_2nd_Edition> [accessed 11 August 2016].

Wakeford, T. and Pimbert, M. (2004) 'Prajateerpu, power and knowledge: the politics of participatory action research in development. Part 2: Analysis, reflections and implications', *Action Research* 2: 25–46.

Wakeford, T. and Pimbert, M. (2013) 'Opening participatory democracy's black box: facilitation as creative bricolage', in T. Noorani, C. Blencoe and

J. Brigstocke (eds), *Problems of Participation: Democracy, commodification and the forms by which we live*, ARN Press, Lewes. Available from: <http://bit.ly/1u9lLPb> [accessed 11 August 2016].

Wakeford, T. and Singh, J. (2008) *Towards Empowered Participation: Stories and Reflections, Participatory Learning and Action* 58 <http://pubs.iied.org/14562IIED.html> [accessed 11 August 2016].

Wakeford, T., Pimbert, M. and Walcon, E. (2015) 'Re-fashioning citizens' juries: participatory democracy in action', in H. Bradbury (ed.), *The SAGE Handbook of Action Research*, 3rd edn, Sage Publications, New York, NY.

Wallace, H. (2001) 'The issue of framing and consensus conferences', *Participatory Learning and Action* 40: 61–3, <http://pubs.iied.org/G01295.html> [accessed 11 August 2016].

About the author

Tom Wakeford is reader in public science and lead practitioner of People's Knowledge at the Centre for Agroecology, Water and Resilience, Coventry University, UK.

Glossary

Depending on the different cultural and linguistic contexts in which they are applied, these terms may have alternative (and perhaps more accurate) interpretations to the working definitions listed here. As we ourselves have not necessarily reached a final consensus, they are merely intended to act as a prompt for further reflection and discussion. A further reading list is available at <http://www.peoplesknowledge.org/resources>.

Action research – research that is carried out with the explicit intention of action being taken towards social or organizational change. This contrasts with research carried out for purely academic purposes. Generally an action research process involves cycles of action, reflection on one's own practice, followed by further action (see Chapter 11, 'Signposts for people's knowledge').

Adult education – the ongoing and (usually) voluntary pursuit of knowledge for either personal or professional reasons. Also known as lifelong learning.

Agency – the capacity, condition, or state of acting or of exerting power.

Appreciative inquiry – collective inquiry into the best of what exists. This is usually undertaken in order to imagine what could be, followed by collective design of, a desired future.

Astro-turfing – the partly or wholly fraudulent attempt by big organizations to make it seem as if their campaign has support from a broad spectrum of people at the *grassroots* (see below).

Bricolage – a way to learn and solve problems by trying, testing, playing around. It is taken from a French term referring to the craft skill of creating something from a diverse range of things that happen to be available.

Bricoleur – someone who undertakes *bricolage* (see above).

Citizen science – a form of research covering a spectrum of levels of people's involvement, from merely contributing to research wholly organized by professional scientists (thus closely resembling *scientism*) to people being in charge of forming the questions that are asked, how they are answered and what is done with them (sometimes called 'extreme citizen science' or *participatory action research*).

Co-design – a process of people actively involved in design, usually alongside formally trained designers.

Cognitive justice – coined by Shiv Visvanathan to call for the recognition of decolonized forms of knowledge, sometimes referred to as alternative sciences.

He argues that different knowledges are connected with different livelihoods and lifestyles and should therefore be treated equally.

Collectivity – individuals who are considered as a whole group. An example of collectivity is a gathering of all the people in a particular area.

Coloniality – refers to the interrelationship of the practices and legacies of European colonialism in social orders and forms of knowledge, advanced in postcolonial studies and Latin American *subaltern* studies.

Community-based participatory research – a partnership approach to research that aims to equitably involve community members, organizational representatives, and researchers in all aspects of the research process, and in which all partners contribute expertise and share decision-making and ownership. See *participatory action research*.

Conscientization – achieving an in-depth understanding of the world, allowing for the perception and exposure of social and political contradictions. Also includes taking action against the oppressive elements in one's life that are illuminated by that understanding. Also known as critical consciousness.

Co-option – a process whereby a powerful initiative (or group) subsumes or assimilates a smaller or weaker initiative with related values or interests. It can take place through a process whereby a powerful group gains 'converts' from a smaller group by seeming to adopt key aspects of the latter's interests, without actually adopting the full programme or ideals of the smaller group. There are many accounts of participatory initiatives or methodologies that are initially idealistic, but which are then co-opted by powerful vested interests, becoming tokenistic (see *tokenism*).

Co-production – people actively involved in knowledge production, usually alongside formally trained researchers.

Critical pedagogy – a philosophy of education and social movement that combines education with critical theory. It has been developed as an educational movement to help students develop consciousness of freedom, recognize authoritarian tendencies, and connect knowledge to power and the ability to take constructive action. At the time of writing, the open-source Wikipedia entry on Paulo Freire, the father of critical pedagogy, had inserted the word 'Communist' in front of the first two uses of critical pedagogy, which gives a hint of the controversy aroused by the approach in some circles.

Critical thinking – clear, rational thinking involving critique. A prerequisite for undertaking *critical pedagogy* (see above).

Cultural imperialism – the cultural aspects of imperialism. *Imperialism* is here referring to the creation and maintenance of unequal relationships between civilizations, favouring the more powerful civilization.

Decolonization – decolonization not only refers to the complete removal of the domination of non-indigenous forces within the geographical space and different institutions of the colonized, but also to the decolonizing of the mind from the colonizer's ideas: the ideas that made the colonized seem inferior.

Democratization of knowledge – the bringing of knowledge, and the processes whereby knowledge is generated and its meaning understood, under greater democratic control.

Development – the process of developing, growing and directing change. Often used as a shorthand for economic development – a policy intervention endeavour aimed at bringing about economic and social well-being of people. Who decides how such 'economic and social well-being' is defined, and when a country or its people are 'developed', are matters of major controversy. Some people consider former European colonies to be 'underdeveloped', assuming that the ideal economic and social model is that of former colonial or current neocolonial powers that dominate Europe and North America.

Dialogic – relating to dialogue, which is a written or spoken conversational exchange between two or more people, and a literary and theatrical form that depicts such an exchange. A holistic concept of dialogue embraces multidimensional, dynamic, and context-dependent processes of creating meaning (see *egalitarian dialogue*).

Diffidence – meekness resulting from a lack of self-confidence.

Educational action research – educational research that is carried out with the intention of action being taken (see *action research* and Chapter 11, 'Signposts for people's knowledge').

Egalitarian dialogue – a dialogue in which contributions are considered according to the validity of their reasoning, instead of according to the status or position of power of those who make them.

Emergence – something that emerges, rather than already existing.

Epistemic injustice – when professional expertise is supported at the expense of other forms of knowledge. Miranda Fricker, who coined the term, suggests that it is made up of two components: *heuristic injustice* and *testimonial injustice*.

Epistemology – how we come to know something. The systems by which people gain new knowledge or understanding.

Essentialism – the theory or practice of reducing things to their essences. It is the view that, for any specific entity (such as an animal, a group of people, a physical object, a concept), there is a set of attributes which are necessary to its identity and function. It is part of a complex philosophical argument that goes back to Ancient Greek philosophers, such as Plato and Aristotle. As 'essence' may imply permanence, some argue that essentialist thinking tends towards political conservatism and therefore opposes social change. However, essentialist claims have provided useful rallying points for radical politics, including feminist, anti-racist, and anti-colonial struggles.

Eugenics – the set of beliefs and practices that aims at improving the genetic quality of the human population. The modern history of eugenics began in the early 20th century when a popular eugenics movement emerged in the United Kingdom and spread to many countries, including the United States, Canada, and Nazi Germany. The ideology of Nazism brought together elements of anti-Semitism, racial hygiene, and eugenics, and combined them with territorial expansionism with the goal of obtaining more living space for the Germanic people, who were deemed a superior race.

Exclusion – being kept out. Usually used in the context of social exclusion (or marginalization), which is social disadvantage and relegation to the fringe of society. It is a term used widely in Western academic traditions, across disciplines including education, sociology, psychology, politics, and economics.

Gates – your home. Where you live and feel safe.

Global North – used as part of a description of the North–South socio-economic and political divide. Usually made up of countries including the United States, Canada, Western Europe, Australia, and New Zealand (though definitions vary). See *Global South*.

Global South – usually made up of countries including those in Africa, Latin America, and developing Asia, including the Middle East. See *Global North*.

Grassroots – people at the local and/or most basic level rather than at the larger scales of political activity. Grassroots movements and organizations utilize collective action from the local level to effect change at the local, regional, national, or international level.

Hegemony – originally used by the Ancient Greeks to refer to the political, economic, or military predominance or control of one state over another. In the 19th century, hegemony came to denote 'social or cultural predominance or ascendancy; predominance by one group within a society or milieu'.

Heuristic injustice – the denial of opportunities to develop greater knowledge. See *epistemic injustice*.

Imperialism – a type of advocacy of empire. Its name originated from the Latin word *imperium*, which means to rule over large territories. Imperialism is a policy of extending a country's power and influence through colonization, use of military force, or other means.

Inclusion – an organizational practice and goal drawing on the sociological notion of inclusiveness. This refers to the political action and personal effort in which different groups or individuals having different backgrounds (like origin, age, race and ethnicity, religion, gender, sexual orientation, and gender identity) are culturally and socially accepted and welcomed.

Inclusive research – an umbrella term encompassing participatory, emancipatory, user-led, and partnership research. See also *participatory action research* and Chapter 11, 'Signposts for people's knowledge'.

Institutions – stable, valued, recurring patterns of behaviour (e.g. 'marriage is an institution'). As structures or mechanisms of social order, they govern the behaviour of a set of individuals within a given community. Institutions are identified with a social purpose, transcending individuals and intentions by mediating the rules that govern living behaviour. Erving Goffman (and to some extent Michel Foucault) discussed 'total institutions' as a place of work and residence where a great number of similarly situated people, cut off from the wider community for a considerable time, together lead an enclosed, formally administered round of life.

Interdisciplinary – the combining of two or more academic disciplines into one activity, such as a research project. It is about creating something new by crossing boundaries, and thinking across them.

Intersectionality – the interconnected nature of social categorizations such as race, class, and gender as they apply to a given individual or group, regarded as creating overlapping and interdependent systems of discrimination or disadvantage.

Management – in businesses and organizations, management is the function that coordinates the efforts of people to accomplish goals and objectives by using available resources efficiently and effectively.

Multiculturalism – the existence, acceptance, or promotion of multiple cultural traditions within a single jurisdiction, usually considered in terms of the culture associated with an ethnic group.

Neocolonialism – the geopolitical practice of using capitalism, business globalization, and cultural imperialism to influence a country, in lieu of either direct military control (*imperialism*) or indirect political control (*hegemony*).

Neoliberalism – the resurgence of 19th-century ideas associated with *laissez-faire* economic liberalism. Beginning in the 1970s and 1980s, its advocates supported extensive economic liberalization policies such as privatization, fiscal austerity, deregulation, free trade, and reductions in government spending in order to enhance the role of the private sector in the economy. Neoliberalism is famously associated with the economic policies introduced by Margaret Thatcher in the United Kingdom and Ronald Reagan in the United States. The transition of consensus towards neoliberal policies and the acceptance of neoliberal economic theories in the 1970s are seen by some academics as the root of financialization, with the financial crisis of 2007–08 one of the ultimate results.

Omerta – a rule or code that prohibits speaking or divulging information about certain activities, especially the activities of a criminal organization (obviously not relating researchers to criminals!).

Ontology – deals with questions concerning what entities exist or may be said to exist, and how such entities may be grouped, related within a hierarchy, and subdivided according to similarities and differences. It is the philosophical study of the nature of being, becoming, existence, or reality, as well as the basic categories of being and their relations.

Organizational development – a field of research, theory, and practice dedicated to expanding the knowledge and effectiveness of people to accomplish more successful organizational change and performance.

Organizational learning – learning in, and by, organizations. See also *organizational development*.

Overseas aid – a voluntary transfer of resources from one country to another. Historically, it has been transferred from former colonial nations to former colonies, though often with targets or conditions that may worsen the lives of many people it is trying to help, rather than improving them.

Participatory action research (PAR) – an approach to research in and by communities that emphasizes participation and action. It seeks to understand the world by trying to change it for the good, particularly those experiencing oppression. PAR emphasizes collective inquiry and experimentation grounded in experience and social history. There are many different traditions of PAR in different cultures and in different languages. See *community-based participatory research* and Chapter 11, 'Signposts for people's knowledge'.

Participatory health research (PHR) – is a recently - coined term describing *participatory research* undertaken by or with formally trained health professionals. It is defined by the International Collaboration on Participatory Health Research as 'action research, engaging people in making change for the better, for example, by finding ways to make neighbourhoods safer, helping health professionals to know what patients need, and empowering citizens to take political action to improve their living conditions'.

Participation industry – the often tokenistic use of participatory terminology and tokenistic participatory techniques by commercial or academic researchers for personal or corporate benefit.

Participatory research – a term often not defined at all or used as a shorthand for *community-based participatory research*.

Participatory rural appraisal (PRA) – an approach used by overseas aid organizations and other non-governmental organizations that aims to incorporate the knowledge and opinions of rural people in the planning and management of development projects and programmes. Robert Chambers, a key exponent of PRA, argues that the approach owes much to 'the Freirean theme that poor and exploited people can and should be enabled to analyse their own reality'. However, the rapid expansion of its use and the tendency for it to be applied by people and organizations who were unable (or unwilling) to tackle *structural violence* led to many criticisms. The term is now rarely used in practice.

Patient involvement – a broad term referring to the communication with patients by those with power or expertise in the health system. This might be for the purpose of improving their immediate care or conducting medical research.

Pedagogy – the discipline that deals with the theory and practice of education; it concerns the study and practice of how best to teach. See *critical pedagogy*.

Policy – a principle of behaviour or conduct that is thought to be desirable or necessary, especially as formally expressed by a government or other power holder.

Post-racial – the idea that a society is free from racial preference, discrimination, and prejudice.

Public engagement – a broad term referring to those with power or expertise engaging in communication with broader society.

Public science – research that is conducted amongst, or includes, the public. Two traditions of public science have emerged, one based on *participatory action research* and another based on outreach programmes by scientists and science communicators.

Recidivism – a repeated relapsing into criminal or delinquent behaviour.

Reflexivity – a term with several meanings. In participatory work it often refers to the ability of the researcher to reflect on their actions. It also refers to people's attempt to recognize the forces that may alter their place in the social structure (e.g. 'I am more likely to be treated as an expert in my organization because I am a white man').

Representation – describes how some individuals stand in for others or a group of others, usually for a certain time period.

Scientism – the over estimation of the importance of physical science, and the belief that it offers the answers to all our worst difficulties. Based on the statements of prominent believers in scientism, Mary Midgley has suggested that the principles of scientism are: all questions of philosophy are either meaningless or can be answered by science; science has authority because it is based on empirical evidence – scientific claims will therefore always overrule philosophical claims; and science provides the ultimate account of the basis of reality – the ultimate metaphysics – but it substantively changes the questions, getting to the correct ones, rather than the meaningless philosophers' ones.

Single regeneration budget – a fund launched in the 1990s in the UK, supposedly to address issues of social and economic deprivation.

Social engagement – the extent to which an individual participates in a broad range of social roles and relationships.

Social justice – justice in terms of the distribution of wealth, opportunities, and privileges within a society.

Structural violence – refers to situations where neither culture nor pure individual will is at fault; rather, historically given – and often economically driven – processes and forces conspire to constrain individual *agency*. Structural violence is visited upon all those whose social status denies them access to the fruits of new knowledge or to benefits enjoyed by others.

Subaltern – refers to the populations that are socially, politically, and geographically outside the dominant power structure of the colony and of the colonial homeland. Usually used in the context of colonialism or *neocolonialism*.

Technological determinism – the idea that the future is determined by the technologies available to it, rather than the power of humans to shape it.

Testimonial injustice – where expertise derived through life experience, rather than professional training, is typically sidelined (see *epistemic injustice*).

Tokenism – a policy of formally complying with efforts to achieve a goal by making small, token gestures, even though they do not contribute significantly towards reaching that goal.

Transdisciplinary – a contested term, which is often used to refer to the undertaking of new approaches in research (such as *participatory action research*) in situations where the very nature of a problem is under dispute.

Transformative – leading to a transformation.

Triple-loop learning – where the process of learning is, itself, the object of learning (see *reflexivity*).

Index

Abroad Again: On the Brandwagon (film) 78
academic and community partnerships 13–14, 25–6, 28–9, 128
'action research' 118
Adichie, Ngozi 39–40, 42, 43
agency and communality 68–9
anti-racism *see* post-racist society
Arendt, Hannah 1, 3
Army and Navy Stores, Liverpool 84
Arts Council, Manchester 88
Arts and Humanities Research Council (AHRC)
 co-design programme 23
 Connected Communities events and festivals 26, 70
 Connected Communities programme 12, 24, 27
 Connected Communities Summit 25
 Remaking Society 75
 Web of Connections 63, 65, 67, 68, 71
Asian community and far-right political groups (citizens' jury) 124–5
Austin Smith Memorial Small Grants Fund 91
authenticity in co-produced research 63–72

Baxter, H. and Cosslett, R.L. 38, 43
Becoming a Londoner 67
Bhambra, G.K. 47
Biko, Steve 1
biological determinism 46
Black Panther Party 83–4

black participatory research (BPR) 115, 117
Black Studies 85
Boyz n the Hood (film) 49–50
Brah, A. and Phoenix, A. 39
Brazil (citizens' jury) 122
bricolage 119
British Medical Journal 97
Brookfield, S.D. 25
business action research (BAR) 115–16, 117

capacity to care 127
Carr, W.S. and Kemmis, S. 25
cheerleaders in partnership proposals 15
choices, awareness and consequences of 67–8
citizen science 109, 110
citizen scientists, Haiti 103–12
citizens' juries 118–26
'Citzen Foresight' 120
civil rights activist's reflections, Liverpool 83–6
 Granby Toxteth Review (GTR) 86–91, 92
 showing lack of social justice 86
 value of co-produced research 91–2
collaborative research/partnerships 13–14, 25–6, 28–9, 128
colonialism 2
 and decolonizing minds 49
 Haiti 103–12
 and racism 46, 47, 129
Coloured folk are so colourful (poem) 55–7
communality and agency 68–9

communicative space for dialogue
66–7
community and academic
partnerships 13–14, 25–6,
28–9, 128
community engagement 30, 31
community media, Tyneside 73–6
backlash against participatory and
community arts 78–9
future promise of 81
and Millennium Bridge 79–80
research method: issues and
problems 76–8
The Coming Age of We (poem) 59–62
Coote, A. and Lenaghan, J. 119–20
co-produced research 14, 63, 83,
91-92
Cordner, A. et al. 127–8
critical action research traditions
115–17
critical thinking/reflection 71, 129
framing questions 25
obstacles to 21

decolonizing minds 49
diversity 30
Douglas, C. 70
Downer, Jackie 16

educational action research (EAR)
115, 116, 117
Eichmann, Adolf 7
empathic imagination 69
ethical principles and practice 126–8
events
attending 29–30
Connected Communities 26, 70
expert patient role 97

famine, Zimbabwe (citizens' jury) 123
Famine (PAR) (poem) 57–8
Fanon, Frantz 49, 83
far-right political groups 47
and Asian community (citizens'
jury) 124–5

'fast capitalism' and 'fast science'
118–19
feelings, turning into
learning 70–1
feminist perspective *see* 'Women's
Circle'
film/film-making
race representations 49–50
Women's Circle 34
see also community media,
Tyneside
Francis Inquiry 127
Freire, Paulo 68, 77, 114
Horton, M. and 30
Fricker, Miranda 1, 120
Froggett, Lynn 127
Fuller, Steve 118–19
funders/funding 3, 14–16
citizens' juries 123, 124, 127
Granby Toxteth Review (GTR) 87,
88, 90–1
minority perspective 49
UK-PBC Consortium 97–8

Genetics Forum (citizens' jury)
119–20
Germany 118
Ginwright, S. 31
Giroux, H. 8
Gormley, Anthony 119
Granby Toxteth Review (GTR)
86–91, 92

Haiti
history 105–9
citizen scientists 105–12
Harris, Leonard 25
hierarchies 1–2
of needs 68
of race 46
Holzkamp, Klaus 118
hooks, b. 28, 38–9, 41
Horton, M. and Freire, P. 30
Humanah Youth, Middlesborough
23, 64, 68

India: citizens' juries 120–2
institutional racism 47, 86, 91
institutions, power of 31
interdependence of 'me', 'us', and
    'the world' 69–70
internalized sexism 41–2
'international art English' 78–9
international development charities
    (citizens' juries) 120–3
intersectionality 39–41
Islamophobia 47

James, Professor Oliver 95
Jeffery, Graham 75
Jones, Professor David 96–7, 98,
    99, 100
journalism: *Granby Toxteth Review*
    (GTR) 86–91, 92
justice and knowledge 1–4

Kashefi, Elham 125
Kemmis, S. 68
    Carr, W.S. and 25
King, Martin Luther 69
Klein, Josephine 69

Lafleur, Michael 103, 104, 105, 106,
    108, 109, 111
language
    'action research' 118
    jargon 114–15
    local 121, 122
    power of words 27–8, 30
Latin America 118
Lawrence, Stephen 47, 91
leadership and participants 15
learning, turning feelings into 70–1
legitimacy though engagement 67, 68
LIVErNORTH
    diagnosis 93–5
    expert patient role 97
    participation in research 95–8
    'patient and public involvement'
        (PPI) 99–100
    reflections 98–100

Liverpool *see* civil rights activist's
    reflections
Luther King, Martin 69

Macpherson, W. 47
Maguire, Patricia 126
Marshall, J. 68, 69
Maslow, A. 68
Meades, Jonathan 78
Mid-Staffordshire hospital scandal 127
Midgley, Mary 110
Millennium Bridge, Tyneside 79–80
Moores, Sir John 88

neoliberalism 110, 118–19
Newton, Professor Julia 97, 98

older people (citizens' jury) 123–4
Oxford University: *Refugee Voices*
    conference 12

painting and colonial history, Haiti
    103–12
participatory action research (PAR)
    2, 19, 23, 24, 53, 57, 64-5, 110,
    113,115, 116–17, 119, 140
patient knowledge *see* LIVErNORTH
'patient and public involvement'
    (PPI) 99–100
Pearson, L. et al. 27
people's knowledge 53, 110,
    113–14, 128
People's Knowledge Editorial
    Collective 1–4
Perry, Grayson 78–9
persistence 30
poems 53–62
police: institutional racism 47,
    86, 91
post-racist society 45, 50–1
    and racism 46–7
    racism and research 47–8
    reflections from practice 49–50
    responding to challenges of 48–9
Poverty - It's a Crime (film) 76–7

poverty and exclusion *see*
  community media, Tyneside
power 29
  challenging 24–5
  of institutions 31
  of people's knowledge 114–19
  of self 30
  of words 27–8, 30
primary biliary cirrhosis 93
proposals
  partnership 15
  research 25–6, 29, 64
pseudo-participation 122

Race Equality News (magazine) 87
race as experience 48
Race Relations Act (1965) 85
racism
  and colonialism 46, 47, 129
  institutional 47, 86, 91
  and sexism 43
  see also civil rights activist's
    reflections, Liverpool; far-right
    political groups; post-racist
    society
Reason, P. 63–4, 66, 67, 69
  and Bradbury, H. 71, 126
'reflexive research ethics' 127–8
Refugee Voices conference 12
Refugee Study Centre 12
RefugeeYouth 23–4
  advice to academics and academy
    30
  advice to communities 29–30
  challenging power in the 'white-
    walled labyrinth' 24–5
  co-designing research proposal
    and submission 25–6
  entering academic spaces 26–7
  framing critical questions 25
  participatory research
    approach 24
  power of words 27–8, 30
  working with academic
    partners 28–9

writing a paper 27–8
  see also authenticity in
    co-produced research;
    'Women's Circle'
Remaking Society (film) 75–6
research proposals 25–6, 29, 64
Rorty, R. 66, 69
Royal Society of Sciences and Art,
  Saint Domingue 105, 107

safe environment 37–9
Said, Edward 47
Saint Domingue (Haiti) 105
Sayyid, S. 46, 48
science education (citizens' jury) 125
scientism 109–10, 128
self, power of 30
sexism *see* 'Women's Circle'
signposts for people's knowledge
  113–14
  citizens' juries 118–26
  ethical principles and practice
    126–8
  power map of people's knowledge
    114–19
  young scientist's letter to self
    128–9
slavery 105, 107–9
Smith, Barbara 41
Smith, S.E. and Colin III, S.A.J. 27
Social Exclusion Game 90
social justice 13–14
social media 86
Spivak, G. and Harasym, S. 47, 49
Stag, Professor 20
Stark, Peter 78
The Struggle (poem) 54–5
Swingbridge Media 73–6, 77–8,
  79–80

Tackling Poverty (film) 74, 81
tokenism 15
Toxteth *see* civil rights activist's
  reflections, Liverpool
Tuhiwai Smith, Linda 2, 47

Tyneside *see* community media,
    Tyneside

UK Government
    and far-right groups 47
    science department 125
    and World Bank investment plan,
        India 121–2
UK-PBC Consortium 97–8, 99
universities 11–12
    collaborative research/
        partnerships 13–14, 25–6,
        28–9, 128
    funder perspective 14–16
    Glastonbury and goldfish 16–17
    obstacles to critical thinking 21
    purpose of 19–21
    Refugee Voices conference 12
    and RefugeeYouth 26–7, 28–9, 30
    research and practice dichotomy
        18–19

rules 17–18
    shared ideas 19
user view 16

Vision 2020 development plan,
    India (citizens' jury) 121–2
Visvanathan, Shiv 2

white male privilege 129
'Women's Circle' 33–4
    challenging sexism 42–4
    commonality of sisterhood 37–9
    internalized sexism 41–2
    intersectionality 39–41
    necessity of women's spaces 35–7,
        42, 44
    Our Journey (film) 34
words, power of 27–8, 30

Zimbabwe (citizens' jury) 123